WILD
HONEY
& RYE

REN BEHAN

WILD
HONEY
& RYE

MODERN
POLISH
RECIPES

Interlink Books

I dedicate this book to my Mama, Alicja, with whom I am fortunate to share everything, including a love of good Polish food, and who continues to pass on that heritage to me.

And to my late father, Longin "Leon" Marczak, who passed away during the year I began writing this book and who was so very proud to be Polish.

CONTENTS

INTRODUCTION

"If you're curious about the world, then food is a wonderfully satisfying way of approaching it because all human experience can be investigated through the food that appears on your plate— there's always a story." **Matthew Fort**

A love of good food and pride in my Polish heritage are the two things that inspired me to write this book. When I first started writing about food six years ago, after a fairly bold leap from the courtroom as a criminal lawyer into the family kitchen as a new mother, I had no big plan, other than to weave a little more creativity into my life and to find ways to make the task of feeding my family something more inspiring than an everyday chore. This leap opened up many new doors and I now spend every day doing what I love: cooking, trying new recipes, writing about food, traveling (when time allows), experiencing new food adventures, and feeding my family. I don't believe that there is any secret formula to being a good cook and I am very much against prescriptive styles of cooking. Yes, cookbooks and television programs can guide you, but there's no substitute for simply getting into the kitchen and experimenting.

These days, we are constantly exposed to new flavors and to new cuisines, particularly via the medium of the internet, and it is perhaps as a result of this explosion in "online food tourism" that we have become more adventurous and more willing to try something new. The enthusiasm to try the unfamiliar is part of what I hope encouraged you to buy, borrow, or read this book. Pushing myself to try something new is how I ended up writing it.

POLONIA AND POLISH FOOD

Having been born in England and raised by parents who were post-Second World War émigrés, my heritage has given me a unique perspective into the world of Polish food and culture. Polonia means Poland in Latin, but it is also the term assigned to the Polish diaspora: people of Polish ancestry or origin living outside of Poland around the world. We are a strong collective—one of the largest in the world. I have grown up eating Polish food, whether through the recipes that my maternal grandmother, Babcia Tekla, passed on to my Mama, Alicja, or enjoying a plateful of scrambled eggs with *kiełbasa* (Polish sausage) with snipped chives prepared by my dad, or sitting down to *Wigilia*—our Polish Christmas Eve vigil meal—with at least fifteen others around the table and the traditional spare place for the unexpected guest.

My father, Longin, and his twin, Jeremi (named after two characters in the Henryk Sienkiewicz novel *Ogniem i Mieczem*—"With Fire and Sword"), were just sixteen and living in Poland when the war broke out. Their father, Stanisław, had fought in the Polish–Bolshevik War many years earlier. In 1942, my father, his twin, their younger brother, and my grandfather all fought with the Polish Armed Forces in the West after having been deported three years earlier to the far north Russian region of the Oblast Archangelsk, some 1,700 miles (2,700 km) from eastern Poland. My mother's parents were also deported and sent to work in an Austrian labor camp, only narrowly escaping with their lives. There's no doubt that being forced to leave a country torn apart by war sharpened my parents' nostalgia. Their desire to preserve their memories of Poland was a driving force, perhaps even the key to their survival in a new land, far away from everything they had previously known and loved. I am sure that this is the case for almost anyone who finds themselves displaced—the pull to preserve is stronger when you haven't been given a choice to leave.

I have often caught myself trying to reconcile the very "Polishness" of my upbringing with the British sleeve of my passport. Perhaps if I had been

Clockwise from top left: Ciocia Maryisia, Mama Alicja, Babcia Tekla Wilczek; me, leading a Polish Scout camp in Scotland; with my mom and friend Monica at my confirmation/ *bierzmowanie* at the Polish Church of Divine Mercy, Manchester; in Polish national costume at the Polish Ex-Combatants Club, Manchester; my father, Longin (Leon), in the Polish Armed Forces in the West, WWII; my uncle Jeremi, father Longin, and uncle Tadzik at their joint 90th birthday celebration (in Polish military uniform); Warsaw, circa 1952, (L–R) my father Longin, mother Alicja, and cousins Rysio and Jurek outside the Teatr Klasyczny; Dad and me during his 90th birthday celebrations; Polish family wedding, featuring homemade vodka and cakes—my dad is on the far right; earliest photograph of my father's family, the Marczaks, on their farmland in Ułanska Dola, Wołyn, near Targowice, Kresy, in Eastern Poland, "The Borderlands," circa 1925; my father and his twin brother Jeremi in the Pierwsza Dywizja Pancerna—the 1st Armoured Division, WWII, circa 1942.

called Susan, I might have felt less Polish, but being the only "Renatka" in a class of British children did make me stand out a bit. We spoke Polish at home, and on Saturdays we went to Polish school. Sundays were usually spent at Polish church and thereafter at the Polish Ex-Combatants Club, where other Poles gathered and where we took part in recitals marking the Polish Constitution of 3 May 1791, or danced in folk costumes to bring some cheer to our homesick parents and grandparents. And then there was the food: my childhood favorites were *pierogi* with cream cheese, rather than macaroni and cheese.

This upbringing, surrounded by a community of other post-war Polish émigrés who found themselves in exactly the same position as my parents, is what shaped me. Their nostalgia, resolve, courage, and a love of Poland through the good times and the bad has made me who I am today and continues to inspire me. I am proud of my dual-cultural heritage and I wave both the British and Polish flags with equal enthusiasm. Polish blood runs through my veins and yet my home has always been in Britain. Preserving our heritage has enriched me and it has influenced many paths that I have taken in life, from my choice of studies to include Polish, to my decision to read Contemporary Eastern European Studies at the UCL School of Slavonic and East European Studies, to my desire to write about Polish food, and to my travels to Poland, which continue to inspire me to hold on tightly to my roots. Many of my family still live in Poland, and it has always been a great pleasure connecting with them throughout my life and being able to slip into Polish conversation during my visits.

REASONS TO FALL IN LOVE WITH POLISH FOOD

My love of Polish food had always been very personal to me, so I have loved seeing it start to have a wider appeal. In 2014, as part of a campaign for the Polish Ministry of Foreign Affairs entitled "Polska: Spring into New," I wrote an article called "Five Reasons to Fall in Love with Polish Food." I could have given hundreds of reasons, but summed it up in five:

1. Polish food is fresh, vibrant, versatile, and modern. Poland even has a Michelin star (two, now, as a second restaurant won a star in March 2016) and fine dining in Poland is more affordable in comparison with high-end dining in other parts of Europe. Street food and festivals are springing up all over Poland and the contemporary food scene is thriving.

2. Polish food can be vegetarian, vegan, and gluten-free, too. Who knew? I even saw a "vegan tartare" on the menu in one trendy eatery—although, fear not, you can still get plenty of amazing quality, high-welfare meat. Fresh produce is widely celebrated and there has been a revival of interest in food markets and growing your own vegetables, herbs, and fruit.

3. Traditional Polish food will keep you warm in the winter. This is true, but while *kuchnia staropolska*, or old Polish cooking, is still very much present in Poland—and many of my favorite family recipes are based upon this type of cooking—it has been brought bang up to date. I have enjoyed experimenting with some of my most-trusted family recipes and in some cases have been able to lighten them up or speed up the cooking time to make them more practicable for today's lifestyles.

4. Polish food has taken influences from many global cuisines—which means that many dishes have their roots in Italian, French, and Scandinavian cooking, as well as from the Turkish spice trading routes and from various border shifts around Eastern Europe. When the Italian noblewoman Bona Sforza came to Poland to marry King Sigismund I in 1518, she brought with her Italian cooks who planted vegetable gardens at the castle in Wawel. Queen Bona was said to have introduced foods such as oranges, lemons, figs, asparagus, artichokes, tomatoes, and pomegranates. This is why many vegetables in Poland take their names from their Italian counterparts: the word for tomatoes in Polish is *pomidory*, which comes from the Italian *pomodoro*, and the word for cauliflower, which in Polish is *kalafior*, comes from the Italian *cavolfiore*. During the 19th century, Polish émigrés to Paris even managed to influence the French: a number of recipes are described as "à la Polonaise," meaning "in the Polish style."

5. Polish food—especially Polish herrings (*śledzie*), charcuterie (*wędliny*), and many types of *zakąski*, or small bites—goes particularly well with vodka. The popularity of Polish vodka worldwide is undisputed and I have dedicated a chapter of this book to the art of making Polish flavored vodkas (page 186). Vodka has been produced in Poland since the early Middle Ages. Today, in order to receive the stamp of guaranteed Polish vodka, it must be produced exclusively in Poland, from traditional cereals—rye, wheat, or barley—or from potatoes. My favorite is rye vodka.

The article I wrote, sharing a few light-hearted suggestions as to why you might fall in love with Polish food, received 27,000 likes and shares across social media in just three weeks. I'd been eating Polish food my whole life and had shared a few of my family recipes through my food writing, and spoken about Polish food on the radio. Was there really anything new to say about Polish cuisine? I went back to some earlier ideas I'd had about writing a Polish heritage-inspired cookbook. I asked more questions of family and friends. I began the process of writing down the recipes that my Mama had passed on to me, challenging myself to try the more unusual ones that hadn't formed part of my everyday repertoire. I experimented with ingredients from my local Polish shop and made them laugh with my grammatically incorrect requests—for anyone who doesn't speak Polish, don't ever underestimate the complicated nuances of the Polish language!

CHANGING PERCEPTIONS

In 2015, seven months after my father passed, I returned to Poland and suddenly there was a sharpness and a clarity that I had not experienced before. Presented with the opportunity of returning with a couple of friends, who had also grown up with Polish parents in Manchester, I hopped on a plane, not expecting to experience anything particularly different to my previous trips to Poland. I went back to some of the places that I had visited in my twenties during a research stint at the Institute of Political Science in Warsaw as part of my undergraduate dissertation on Poland's role in NATO. I visited my Polish cousins, supported my friend who was taking part in a race though Warsaw on Independence Day, and I felt an urge to pay my respects at the monument to the regiment in which my father had served during the Second World War—the Polish 1st Armored Division, or *1 Dywizja Pancerna*. It was a pilgrimage of sorts, and while I expected it to be emotional, I hadn't expected Poland to make such an impression on me. There is no doubt that this particular visit to Warsaw changed my perceptions of modern life and culture in Poland today.

I found that Poland had changed. She had moved on and there was a completely new air of hope. There were city-center food markets and breakfast markets and food tours and vodka tours. Warsaw was exciting, modern, cosmopolitan. We drank cocktails in trendy bars, I ate *bigos* and pastry rolls filled with sauerkraut and mushrooms at a food market by the old town, we tried local Polish wine, and I found flavors of *pierogi* that I had never tried before. Polish hospitality, which I grew up experiencing in England and during vacations to Poland, was just as it had always been—except that at my cousin Joasia's house we drank Polish vodka and ate French patisserie that she had grabbed on her way home from work before she ran off to her salsa class!

I realized that this is the Poland I wanted to share in my book. Not the Poland of our past, but the Poland of our present and, I hope, of our future. My aim is to introduce you to Polish food in a new way—perhaps you have visited Poland or may do so in the future, perhaps you have a Polish neighbor or a colleague at work (highly likely), perhaps you are simply inspired to give one or two of my recipes a try.

You'll find that the recipes in this book use widely available ingredients, with an emphasis on seasonal fruits and vegetables, as well as a selection of healthy grains. Occasionally, sourcing some of the ingredients, such as smoked Polish hams or *twaróg*, a type of soft white cheese, may involve a trip to your local Polish deli, but many supermarkets now sell Polish food.

Left: Der Elefant restaurant, Plac Bankowy, Warsaw.

The Polish pantry section (page 18) will help you out. Don't feel like you're breaking the rules by swapping a can of traditional Polish sauerkraut for a modern, organic version from your local health food store.

Should you ever find yourself visiting Poland, I hope you'll be encouraged to join in a Polish food and vodka tour, or even a supper club, for an alternative cultural experience. Most cities offer food tours, and there are many street food festivals popping up. I particularly recommend the annual Pierogi Festival in Krakow (the *Festiwal Pierogów,* which takes place every August). There are also plenty of regional Easter festivals around Poland, which offer a beautiful insight into Polish culture, and a trip to the region of Małopolska, where my maternal grandfather was born and where much of my family lived, is always a treat filled with honey festivals; the Krakow Honey Harvest in September is a must—and inspired the name of this book.

Smacznego!

REN BEHAN

"Know from whence you came.
If you know whence you came, there
are absolutely no limitations to
where you can go." **James Baldwin**

Right: Wild honey vodka and rye bread, Dom Wódki (House of Vodka), Warsaw.

Scenes from the breakfast markets, *Targ Śniadaniowy*, Warsaw.

THE POLISH PANTRY

I'm sure that you'll have no problem sourcing the ingredients for the recipes within this book, and where possible I have given alternatives. Here are some of the key ingredients that you'll find in a Polish kitchen.

FROM THE GARDEN

BAY LEAVES—LIŚCIE LAUROWE
Fresh and dried bay leaves can be used interchangeably—we have a small bay tree in the garden, so I tend to use fresh.

BEET STALKS/GREENS—BOTWINA
In the summer months you often see beets with stalks and leaves attached. Don't throw these away—instead, chop them finely and add them to soups.

CHIVES—SZCZYPIOREK
Many Polish savory recipes suggest "sprinkling with chives." Always use fresh chives and chop them finely, using a sharp knife. Once chopped, they can be frozen.

DILL—KOPEREK
The Poles use plenty of fresh and dried dill and I would say this is the dominant herb in Polish cooking. My grandmother had an abundance of dill growing in her garden and it appears in many Polish dishes, for example in salads, on potatoes, in soups, as a garnish on sandwiches, with eggs, and on meat and fish. Fresh dill can be chopped and frozen, which I find is a slightly better option than using dried dill. If you really don't like dill, use fresh parsley instead.

HORSERADISH—CHRZAN
The Poles serve horseradish (usually a creamy horseradish sauce) with smoked sausages. Fresh horseradish is a root that looks similar to parsnip. It has a peppery flavor and is related to mustard. If you can find fresh horseradish, peel it and finely grate it before adding it to dishes, or mix it with mayonnaise. You can also buy horseradish cream to serve with smoked meats.

MARJORAM—MAJERANEK
Marjoram is very popular in Polish cooking, and is lovely with roast chicken. It is simple to grow your own on the kitchen windowsill, or you can use dried marjoram.

PARSLEY—PIETRUSZKA ZIELONA
Natka pietruszki are parsley leaves. Use fresh parsley whenever possible, ideally flat-leaf parsley. You can chop the fresh leaves and freeze them.

SORREL—SZCZAW
Sorrel grows abundantly in Poland and is often used to make sorrel soup. My mama makes it often during the summer months and I love it. However, unless you grow it yourself, you may struggle to find fresh sorrel, so I haven't included a sorrel soup recipe. It's simple to make: all you have to do is add chopped fresh sorrel to a chicken or vegetable stock. Stir in a little cream and lemon juice and serve the soup garnished with chopped hard-boiled eggs.

FROM THE PANTRY

ALLSPICE—ZIELE ANGIELSKIE
Use whole allspice berries: these are the dried, unripe fruit of a Caribbean plant, and they look similar to large black peppercorns. They are used to flavor stews, such as *bigos* and *gulasz*, and can be used when pickling cucumbers, too.

ANISE—ANYŻ
Anise and star anise aren't traditional Polish ingredients but they appear occasionally. I use star anise to flavor carrots (page 92) and to garnish a Polish plum martini (page 199).

CARAWAY SEEDS—KMINEK
Caraway seeds are actually tiny dried fruit, rather than seeds. In the Polish kitchen, caraway is used to flavor bread, *kabanos* sausage, and vegetables such as carrots and cabbage.

CINNAMON—CYNAMON
Cinnamon goes into apple cakes, Christmas cookies, and *krupnik*—Polish honey vodka.

PEPPER—PIEPRZ
Pepper in Polish cooking is black pepper. I prefer to use freshly ground black pepper, not the very finely ground kind.

VANILLA—WANILIA
Vanilla is a popular flavoring in Polish desserts, cakes, and baked goods. You can use liquid vanilla extract or vanilla bean paste; I prefer to use the paste, or organic vanilla powder, which gives your dessert tiny black speckles.

VEGETABLE SEASONING—VEGETA
This is vegetable bouillon powder made with carrot, parsnip, onion, parsley, and salt. The Poles often add a little pinch to savory dishes (soups, sauces, stews, etc.) for extra flavor, or you can dissolve 1 teaspoon of the powder in 2 cups/500 ml boiling water and use it as a vegetable stock. There is a "Natur" version which has no monosodium glutamate (MSG) or artificial additives.

FATS AND OILS—TŁUSZCZE I OLEJE
The Poles rarely use olive oil (although I tend to use it in salad dressings). Instead, they use vegetable oil—predominantly canola oil or sunflower oil. Lard or pork fat are called for in some traditional recipes; Poles sometimes eat pork fat as a sandwich spread—it's actually very tasty! My preferred oil is a cold-pressed organic canola oil. When preparing herrings (page 99), I recommend cold-pressed linseed (flaxseed) oil.

FLOUR—MĄKA
Wheat flour is generally called *mąka pszenna*. "00" flour or pasta flour is called *mąka tortowa* (cake flour) and may be labeled as "typ 450." Bread flour is *mąka chlebowa* or "typ 750." Wholewheat flour is *mąka razowa* or "typ 2000." So the higher the number or "typ," the less refined the grain.

Rye flour is *mąka żytnia* (sometimes labeled *mąka żytnia razowa*—wholegrain rye flour). In my honey and rye loaf (page 26), I like to use an organic stoneground rye flour from my local mill in Poland. Organic flour may be labeled *mąka ekologiczna*. *Mąka orkiszowa* is spelt flour. Some recipes also call for potato flour, which is *mąka ziemniaczana* — this is a very fine flour and is often used in cakes. Gluten-free flour is known as *mąka bezglutenowa*.

GRAINS AND GROATS—ZIARNA I KASZE

Poland is very rich in agricultural land and has plentiful amounts of grains and cereals, the most common being wheat, rye, and barley. Polish bread is traditionally made with rye, as is Polish vodka.

Groats (kasza, plural kasze) are the hulled grains, which usually, though not always, include the germ and bran. Groats are often used in Polish cooking, the two main varieties being barley (jęczmień) and buckwheat (gryka). Outside Poland, "kasha" is often used to mean buckwheat, particularly in the US, but in Polish cooking kasze covers a far wider range of grains, which can be added to soups, served as an alternative to rice or used in place of risotto rice to make a "kaszotto." A selection of grains will be available at most Polish shops or online; the following are some of the most useful:

Barley

Barley groats—*kasza jęczmienna perłowa*—are what I use most often, for salads, in soups, and as a side dish. Barley groats can be cracked or crushed, fine, medium, or coarse. Check the package for cooking times: most cook in 15 minutes in the same way as rice.

Hulled pearl barley—*kasza jęczmienna pęczak*—whole, shelled, and polished barley seed (with a longer cooking time than the cracked and crushed versions). I use this to make Pearl barley risotto with bacon and roasted pumpkin (page 124).

Buckwheat—*kasza gryczana* or *kasza gryczana biała*

Toasted/roasted buckwheat—*kasza gryczana prażona*

Millet—*kasza jaglana*

Oat—*kasza owsiana*—oat groats are whole, hulled grains, not the rolled or steel cut oats that are common in the US.

Spelt—*kasza orkiszowa*

HONEY—MIÓD

The Poles love honey. Whenever my father felt a sniffle he would make a Polish hot toddy with lemon tea, vodka, and honey. It always seemed to work like a charm in fending off germs—he lived to be over 90! Honey has been used in Polish cooking for centuries: in honey cakes, in honey vodka (*krupnik*), and in traditional Polish mead—a type of beer made with honey. I use honey for drizzling over cream cheese on rye bread, for basting spare ribs and carrots, and in many breads and cakes. In Poland, you can buy lots of different types of honey, including buckwheat honey, dandelion honey, and acacia honey. Raw and organic honeys are gaining popularity and beekeeping is making a comeback, particularly wild beekeeping (where the bees make their hives in tree hollows).

Hunting for wild honey was popular in Poland during the 16th and 17th centuries, and was considered to be a profession that passed from father to son. During the 19th century, the practice of honey hunting died out across most of Europe, surviving only among the Bashkirs of the Ural Mountains. In 2007, wild bees were reintroduced to Polish forests and with the help of Bashkir honey hunters, new generations are being trained in the art of wild beekeeping. Today, in the region of Małopolska, particularly around the town of Nowy Sącz, wild honey hunting is being revived and there are many wild honey festivals.

For the recipes in this book, you can experiment with any local, organic, or wild honey that you can find.

CARAMEL SAUCE—MASA KRÓWKOWA

A caramel made from condensed milk and sugar, similar to dulce de leche. Use this to make the Polish fudge ice cream (page 180) or the caramel and cherry cheesecake (page 181).

Right: Homemade jams, pickles, *nalewki*, and cakes.

FROM THE POLISH DELI

BREAD—CHLEB
Bread in Poland is usually made with a blend of wheat flour and rye flour; it may be made with yeast (*na dr ̇adżach*), or with a sourdough starter (*na zakwasie*). A bread roll is a *bułka*, *bułeczka*, or *buła*. White bread is *biały chleb*, brown bread is *ciemny chleb*, wholewheat bread is *chleb pełn oziarnisty*.

POLISH SOFT WHITE CHEESE—TWARÓG
Also known as *biały ser* (white cheese), farmer's cheese, or curd cheese, *twaróg* is often labeled "farmer's cheese" in the US. If you can't find curd cheese, use cream cheese. There is a very smooth form of *twaróg* called *twaróg mielony* or *twaróg sernikowy*, used for cheesecakes: if you can't find this, you can pass regular *twaróg* through a sieve for a smoother consistency. *Ser wiejski* is cottage cheese.

SOUR CREAM—ŚMIETANA KWAŚNA
Sour cream is used in a number of Polish recipes, both savory and sweet; it is available with different fat contents, most commonly 12% or 18%. *Kremówka* or *śmietanka*, usually with 30% fat, is not sour and can be whipped or added to coffee.

OTHER DAIRY—NABIAŁ
Poles also use buttermilk, *maślanka*, and they drink kefir, a healthy, yogurt-like fermented milk drink.

HERRINGS—ŚLEDZIE
The best type are *matiasy* or *matjas*—young herring fillets with a pink tinge. At the Polish deli, you'll find them in packages—and occasionally in barrels—marinated in oil.

POLISH SAUSAGE—KIEŁBASA
There are probably over a hundred types of Polish sausage. Most Polish sausages are flavored with garlic and they are usually cured and smoked—so they are ready to eat; the recipes in this book call for this type of sausage. In most cases, I use *kiełbasa wiejska*, or farmhouse sausage, which you can either buy in a ring or sliced. *Krakowska*, slightly larger and often sold sliced in packages, is another type I like. Thinner types of Polish sausage are called *kabanosy*. *Parówki* are similar to frankfurters. In the US, kielbasa is commonly available as a type of hot dog sausage. You can also buy raw Polish sausage, so be careful to check; for instance, white sausage (*biala kiełbasa*) is usually uncooked.

POLISH HAM—SZYNKA
There are many types of Polish ham. Look for *szynka babuni*, *szynka wiejska*, or *polędwica sopocka*—a type of cured pork loin.

PICKLED CUCUMBER—OGÓREK KISZONY OR KWASZONY
Pickled cucumbers in Poland are the small variety known as cornichons in the US. *Ogórki kiszone* (the plural of *ogórek kiszony*) are pickled cucumbers in brine (dill pickles). You can also buy sour pickled cucumbers—*kwaśne ogórki*—which are usually pickled in vinegar. My recipe on page 66 uses the brining method, meaning that they are naturally fermented—*małosolne*, or lightly salted. Brined cucumbers do not keep as long as cucumbers pickled in vinegar, so after a short period of fermentation they should be stored in the fridge.

Left: Pickling cucumbers with dill, horseradish root, and garlic.

SWEET AND SAVORY BREAKFASTS

ŚNIADANIE

I'm often asked what a typical Polish breakfast entails and I'm immediately drawn into sharing my experience of the *Targ Śniadaniowy*, the breakfast market in Warsaw, where families and friends gather on weekends to sit communally and enjoy an open-air breakfast or brunch. The concept of local producers getting together to share their offerings isn't new—there are farmers' markets and food festivals all over the world. But what I did find interesting was that this is how Varsovians, old and young, start their weekends—and in huge numbers. The scene has stayed with me—colorful picnic blankets all around, deck chairs and communal tables laid with pretty tablecloths. Everyone is catered for by the array of food on offer—there are vegan tarts, freshly baked bread, Polish cheese, local honey, smoothies, omelets, open sandwiches, and very good coffee. Children take part in cooking classes, giving their parents a chance to sit and chat, or perhaps take part in an open-air yoga class. Other breakfast markets are springing up in cities across Poland and it's easy to see why.

At home, I continue to be influenced by the type of breakfast that my Polish parents cooked for me when I was growing up, such as softly scrambled eggs with plenty of Polish sausage, *kiełbasa*, imparting its distinctive smoky, garlicky flavor. Or bread with cream cheese, *twaróżek*, with radish and fresh chives. Nobody should leave the house for work or school on an empty tummy—even a slice of bread with thick plum jam, *powidła*, will suffice. Tea was, and still is, taken with lemon.
I find myself experimenting more and more with Polish ingredients now that they are so readily available—perhaps adding slices of *kabanos* (a smoked cured sausage) to eggs, which I bake in the oven along with spinach and tomatoes or a handful of mushrooms. This becomes a Polish version of a North African *shakshuka* or Spanish baked eggs with chorizo, but with the flavor of caraway from the *kabanos*.

This chapter offers ideas for a healthy start to the day, to give you a taste of what breakfast in Poland is like today.

Left: Breakfast markets, *Targ Śniadaniowy*, Warsaw.

HONEY AND RYE LOAF

CHLEB ŻYTNI Z MIODEM

I have to confess that I am not a regular baker of bread, though it is a skill I would love to incorporate into daily life. I particularly like sourdough breads and most Polish bread begins with a *zakwas*, or sourdough starter. This simple honey and rye loaf, however, is for times when I just want to use pantry ingredients. It is particularly good with butter, *twaróg* (Polish soft cheese) or cream cheese and honey, but it is equally good when served with eggs, and it can be toasted. I like to use a mixture of rye and white bread flour, and I also add a sprinkle of caraway seeds, as is traditional in Polish baking; the caraway seeds are optional.

Makes 1 loaf

½ cup/125 ml lukewarm water
½ cup/125 ml lukewarm whole milk
2 tbsp clear honey
¼ oz/7 g (one envelope) active-dry yeast
2½ cups/9 oz/250 g rye flour— or use wholewheat or spelt flour—plus extra for dusting
2 cups/9 oz/250 g white bread flour
½ tsp salt
2 tsp caraway seeds (optional)
1 tsp vegetable oil, for greasing

Mix the water and milk together, add the honey, and stir until dissolved. Tip in the yeast, whisk, and leave to stand in a warm place for 10 minutes.

In a large bowl, combine the flours and salt, and the caraway seeds, if using. Make a well in the center and stir in the liquid yeast mixture until the dough comes together.

Dust your work surface with rye flour. Tip the dough onto the surface and knead it for 10 minutes. Shape the dough into a ball.

Grease a clean bowl with oil and put the dough into the bowl. Cover with plastic wrap and leave in a warm place until the dough has roughly doubled in size. This may take up to 2 hours.

Preheat the oven to 400°F/200°C and oil a large baking sheet.

Tip the dough out onto the work surface, knead it briefly, then shape into an oval loaf and place it on the greased baking sheet. Slash the top with a sharp knife and bake for 45 minutes or until it is golden brown all over.

Leave the loaf on a wire rack to cool before slicing.

HOME-INFUSED HONEY

ZIOŁOMIODY

Honey features regularly in Polish recipes—it is considered to be important both medicinally (with anti-inflammatory and anti-bacterial properties) and as a culinary ingredient in traditional recipes such as mead, a type of Polish beer made with honey, *krupnik*, a spiced honey vodka (page 196), and in cakes such as *piernik,* or gingerbread. As a child, I used to drink my tea with lemon and honey and we were always given a spoonful of honey if we had a cough or the beginnings of a cold. These days, I also enjoy a spoonful of honey in a cup of matcha green tea, drizzled over a cream cheese and rye sandwich, or stirred through millet porridge for breakfast. I also love making infused honey, or *ziołomiody*, echoing flavors I tried during a trip to Małopolska, southern Poland.

Use a light, clear, runny honey as your base.

You can flavor your honey with any of the following: orange peel, thyme, rosemary, mint leaves, lavender, dried rose petals, or sliced vanilla beans.

Use 1–2 tbsp of peel/herbs/petals/pods to 1 cup/12 oz/340 g honey—although in the case of herbs, whole sprigs work best, so just add one or two sprigs.

If using fresh herbs, wash and dry them thoroughly.

You will need clean (sterilized—see page 207) dry jars with well-fitting lids. Place the herbs, peel, petals, or vanilla beans into the jars.

Pour in the honey—you can do this through a funnel if it's easier.

Seal the jars and leave for a week or so to allow the flavors to infuse. After this time, you can strain or remove the peel/herbs/petals/pods to prevent the flavor from becoming too strong.

Store the infused honey in a cool, dry place.

SOFT CHEESE WITH HONEY AND WALNUTS ON RYE

KANAPKI Z TWAROŻKIEM, MIODEM I ORZECHAMI WŁOSKIMI

Many Polish recipes make use of *twaróg* or Polish soft white cheese. These days, curd cheese is usually available at the deli counter, although traditionally Poles would make fresh cheese at home from cows' milk curds. In simple dishes like this one, you could use cream cheese, farmer's cheese (dry curd cottage cheese), or any soft, spreadable white cheese. Here, I've sweetened the cheese by stirring through honey.

Serves 4

3½ oz/100 g *twaróg*, farmer's
   cheese, or cream cheese
4 tsp honey, plus 4 tsp for drizzling
2 tsp unsalted butter
4 slices of rye or other bread
3 tbsp walnuts, chopped

In a small bowl, mix the cheese with 4 teaspoons of the honey.

Butter the bread and then spread the cheese mixture over each slice. Drizzle over the remaining honey and sprinkle over the chopped walnuts.

Serving tip
You can top the sweet cheese with jam or a fruit preserve—*dżem* or *konfitura*—or with freshly sliced fruit, such as bananas, nectarines, or raspberries. Try it with *powidła śliwkowe*, Polish plum butter (page 44).

SOFT CHEESE WITH RADISHES AND CHIVES ON RYE

TWAROŻEK ŚNIADANIOWY

Here, the soft white cheese, *twaróg*, is served as a savory breakfast with fresh radishes and chives. I like to add a little plain yogurt to the *twaróg* for a slight tang. My grandmother often used to serve this for breakfast because she grew radishes and chives in her garden.

Serves 4

3½ oz/100 g *twaróg*, farmer's
   cheese, or cream cheese
sea salt and freshly ground
   black pepper
2 tbsp plain yogurt—or use
   buttermilk (*maślanka*) or kefir
4 radishes, finely chopped
¼ cucumber, diced
2 tsp chopped fresh chives
2 tsp unsalted butter
4 slices of rye or other bread

To garnish
1 radish, finely sliced
2 tbsp chopped fresh chives

Season the cheese with a generous amount of salt and pepper—around ½ teaspoon of each.

Stir in the yogurt or buttermilk and mix with a fork. Add the chopped radishes, cucumber, and chives, and stir again.

Butter the bread and then spread the cheese mixture over each slice. Garnish with radish and chives.

AVOCADO WITH SOFT CHEESE AND SLICED BOILED EGGS

KANAPKI Z AWOKADO I JAJKIEM NA TWARDO

Almost everyone these days has a version of avocado toast. I like to mix my avocados with Polish curd cheese (farmer's cheese or dry curd cottage cheese), spread them on rye bread, and then top them with sliced boiled eggs, radishes, and chives—bringing together healthy fats, protein, and grains. Avocados are not a typically Polish ingredient, but they have gained popularity in recent years. My youngest baby enjoyed this as his first finger food.

Serves 4

2 ripe avocados, halved and pitted
2 tbsp *twaróg*, farmer's cheese, or
  cream cheese
juice of ½ lemon
sea salt and freshly ground
  black pepper
4 slices of bread, preferably rye
2 hard-boiled eggs, peeled
  and sliced

To garnish
a handful of fresh radishes, sliced
1 tsp chopped fresh chives
1 tsp flaxseeds (optional)

Scoop the avocado flesh into a small bowl and mash with a fork. Add the cheese and lemon juice, and season well with salt and pepper.

Spread the mixture over the slices of bread (toasted or untoasted). Top with sliced boiled egg and garnish with radish and chives, and flaxseeds, if using.

BAKED EGGS WITH KABANOS, TOMATOES, AND SPINACH

JAJKA ZAPIEKANE Z KABANOSEM, POMIDORAMI I SZPINAKIEM

Kabanos, or *kabanosy* in the plural, is a variety of Polish pork sausage that is usually quite dry in texture, smoked (therefore cooked and ready to eat), and flavored with caraway seeds. They were my favorite snack as a child, grabbed straight from the fridge and eaten with gusto. They can also be eaten hot: when heated, their smoky flavor really comes through. I tend to use *kabanos* in any recipe that calls for chorizo or pancetta, to make Polish versions of many popular Spanish and Italian dishes. If you can't find *kabanosy*, you can use most types of Polish sausage, more generally known as *kiełbasa*. If you are short on time and don't want to use the oven, you can finish cooking the eggs in the pan. I like to serve these baked eggs still in the pan, with plenty of buttered rye bread on the side.

Serves 4

1 tsp vegetable oil
3½ oz/100 g *kabanos*, sliced
  diagonally
½ cup/3 oz/85 g halved cherry
  tomatoes
¾ cup/¾ oz/20 g fresh spinach
4 eggs
freshly ground black pepper
buttered bread, preferably rye,
  to serve

Preheat the oven to 375°F/190°C.

Using a pan that is safe to go into the oven, heat the oil and cook the *kabanos* for 3 minutes, stirring once or twice until the edges start to brown. Add the tomatoes and cook for another 2 minutes, then add the spinach.

Take the pan off the heat and crack in the eggs, leaving a bit of space around the eggs to make them easier to serve. Season with pepper.

Put the pan in the oven and bake, uncovered, for 6–8 minutes, until the whites are set but the yolks are still runny. Alternatively, cover the pan with a lid and cook over low heat for 3 minutes. Serve with buttered bread.

POLISH DELI BREAKFAST BOARD

ZIMNY BUFET ŚNIADANIOWY

This is a Polish version of a continental breakfast spread—the idea being that you set out plenty of cheese, ham, bread, and salad for everyone to help themselves. You'll find a great selection of breakfast items at the Polish deli. I also like to put out some Mixed vegetable salad or *Sałatka jarzynowa* (page 60).

a selection of cold cuts (*wędliny*) and smoked sausages (*kiełbasy wędzone*)

a selection of cheese (*sery*)

hard-boiled eggs, peeled and sliced

fresh tomatoes, cucumbers, and radishes, sliced

rye bread and butter

Arrange all the items on a large wooden board or serving platter. Serve with plenty of rye and butter.

SCRAMBLED EGGS WITH POLISH SAUSAGE

JAJECZNICA

When I was a child, whenever my dad made breakfast for me, he made fried *kiełbasa* with scrambled eggs. Sometimes he would add a little sprinkle of chopped chives just before serving. Any type of smoked Polish sausage is good here; I like to use *wiejska*, which is widely available. The eggs should always be as fresh as possible and served very soft, preferably in the pan at the table, with plenty of fresh bread on the side. You could use duck eggs instead of hen's eggs in this recipe.

Serves 2

2 tsp butter or vegetable oil
1¾ oz/50 g Polish sausage, sliced
2–3 eggs, lightly beaten
1 tsp chopped fresh chives
2 slices of bread, preferably rye,
   to serve

Put a small nonstick frying pan over medium heat and add the butter or oil. Add the sliced sausage and cook for 2 minutes, until it starts to color and crisp.

Pour the eggs into the frying pan. Leave them to set for a minute or two and then gently stir them with a wooden spoon and let them sit again for 30 seconds. Continue, stirring gently, until the eggs are just starting to set.

Remove from the heat, sprinkle with chives, and serve with rye bread.

ONE-PAN POLISH BREAKFAST

ŚNIADANIE NA JEDNEJ PATELNI

This is probably one of my favorite breakfast dishes. I cook it most weekends, especially when we have visitors. It's so easy to adapt and throw together without a great deal of hassle. Use any type of *kiełbasa* or smoked Polish sausage that you can find, such as *wiejska* or *kabanosy*. You could even use bacon.

Serves 4

1 tsp vegetable oil
6–8 slices of Polish sausage,
   or 4 slices of bacon,
   roughly chopped
8 small tomatoes, quartered
8 mushrooms, halved
4 eggs
2 tsp chopped fresh dill or chives,
   to serve

Preheat the broiler to high.

Heat the oil in a frying pan over a medium heat. Add the sausage or bacon and cook for 2 minutes, until it starts to color. Add the tomatoes and mushrooms, reduce the heat, and cook for 5 minutes.

Make sure everything is evenly spread out in the pan. Create some little gaps and crack in the eggs. Cook until the whites are starting to set, then transfer to the broiler (or cover the pan with a lid) and cook for 2 minutes or until the eggs are done to your liking.

Sprinkle with dill or chives. Serve straight away, in the pan.

•

BOILED EGGS, HAM, AND RADISHES

JAJKA NA TWARDO, SZYNKA I RZODKIEWKI

A protein-packed Polish breakfast-in-a-hurry, this is very simple to prepare the night before, and you can take it to work in a lunchbox. Polish smoked ham has a wonderful flavor and the radishes add a little peppery crunch. This breakfast also goes well with the Mixed vegetable salad, *Sałatka jarzynowa* (page 60).

Serves 1

1–2 eggs
3–4 slices of Polish smoked ham or
   sausage, such as *szynka babuni*
   or *Krakowska*
3–4 radishes

If necessary, take the eggs out of the fridge about 20 minutes before you need them so that they reach room temperature. Bring a saucepan of water to a boil. Carefully lower the eggs into the water and boil for exactly 5 minutes. Drain the eggs and plunge into a bowl of cold water.

Peel the eggs and serve them with the ham and whole radishes.

FRUIT SOUFFLÉ OMELET

OMLET SOUFFLÉ Z OWOCAMI

This is the perfect weekend breakfast, especially during the summer months when ripe berries are plentiful. I like to use strawberries, raspberries, and blueberries, but you can top your omelet with any fruit that you like. In Poland, fruit omelets are also sometimes served as dessert, as well as breakfast. Although omelets may not seem very Polish, they were introduced by King John III Sobieski and his French-born queen, who was said to have adored light omelets. She became known as Maria Kazimiera, or "Marysieńka."

Serves 4

4 eggs, separated
2 tsp whole milk or almond milk
1 tsp honey
a handful of mixed berries, such
    as blueberries, raspberries, and
    quartered strawberries, divided
    into two equal portions
1 tsp vegetable oil
2 tbsp confectioners' sugar

Preheat the broiler to high.

Separate the egg whites from the yolks and place the yolks and whites in separate bowls—a very clean, dry, glass or metal bowl should be used for the egg whites.

Whisk the egg yolks with the milk and honey, then stir in half of the fresh fruit.

Using a very clean whisk, beat the egg whites until stiff. Using a metal spoon, fold them into the egg yolk and fruit mixture until the whites are evenly combined.

Heat the oil in an oven-safe frying pan over low heat. Pour in the egg and fruit mixture and cook for 5 minutes until the bottom of the omelet begins to set. Take care that it doesn't burn.

Sift over 1 tablespoon of confectioners' sugar. Place the omelet pan under the hot broiler for 2 minutes until the top is set and golden brown.

To serve, sprinkle over the remaining fresh fruit and dust with the remaining confectioners' sugar.

MILLET PORRIDGE WITH ALMOND MILK

JAGLANKA Z MLEKIEM MIGDAŁOWYM

When made with almond milk, this porridge is both gluten-free and dairy-free. In Poland, millet groats are known as *kasza jaglana* and they are quite widely used. This is a wonderful breakfast served with a drizzle of wild or home-infused honey (pages 28–29) or a spoonful of Quick blueberry compote (see below).

Serves 2

½ cup/3½ oz/100 g millet
  (*kasza jaglana*)
1 cup/250 ml almond milk, plus
  extra if needed
2 tsp honey, plus extra to serve

In a sieve, rinse the millet until the water runs clear, then drain.

Tip the millet into a saucepan and pour in the almond milk. Bring to a boil, then add the honey. Reduce the heat and simmer gently for 15 minutes. If the millet looks too dry at any point, pour in a little extra milk. You may also want to add a little extra milk before serving.

Serve the millet porridge divided between two bowls and drizzle each with honey, or serve with blueberry compote.

•

QUICK BLUEBERRY COMPOTE

KOMPOT Z JAGÓD

This is a quick jam, perfect for topping millet porridge (see above) or serving with fresh rye bread smothered with plenty of butter. You can also make this with strawberries, chopped into quarters. Poland grows and exports both blueberries (*jagody*) and bilberries (*borówki*), which are slightly smaller. At the Polish deli you can often find bilberries in syrup or made into jam. Picking wild bilberries was one of my grandmother's favorite summer pastimes.

Makes 1 small jar

1⅔ cups/9 oz/250 g fresh or frozen
  blueberries or bilberries
2 tbsp honey
1 tsp water

Sterilize a small jam jar (see page 207).

Wash the fruit and tip it into a saucepan. Add the honey and water and cook over low heat for 3–4 minutes, until the berries soften. Leave to cool and then transfer into the jar and seal. It will keep for 3 days in the fridge.

POLISH PLUM BUTTER

POWIDŁA ŚLIWKOWE

In Poland, you'll find thick, concentrated fruit jams or preserves called *powidła*; they can be made from plums (in Poland, they use a variety called *śliwki Węgierki*), as in this recipe, or from cherries or blackberries. Plum butter is often used in Polish recipes. For instance, you'll see it as a filling in gingerbread cake or as a filling for Polish doughnuts, or *paczki*. Only two ingredients are required, plums and sugar: the trick is to cook the plums over very low heat for a very long time until you have a thick paste. Once you have a jar of this on hand, you can also use it to sweeten savory recipes, such as *Bigos* (page 125), or the sauce that accompanies the duck breasts on page 143. At breakfast, try *powidła* with cream cheese on rye bread.

Makes 2–3 jars

4½ lb/2 kg very ripe purple plums
½ cup/3½ oz/100 g sugar

Wash the plums, and halve and pit them. Put them into a large pan over very low heat and cook for 20–30 minutes, or until they are very soft and falling apart.

Rub the plums through a sieve set over a bowl.

Return the plum purée to the pan and stir in the sugar. Bring the mixture to a boil and then reduce the heat to very low. Cook for about 1–1½ hours, stirring regularly so that the mixture doesn't burn. It will become dark purple and so thick that a spoon will stand upright.

Leave the plum butter to cool. While it is cooling, sterilize your jars (see page 207). Fill the jars with the plum butter, and seal. It will keep for up to 3 weeks in the fridge.

SEASONAL AND RAW SALADS

SAŁATKI I SURÓWKI

In Poland, salad is known as either a *sałatka* or a *surówka*, depending on how it is made. A lettuce is a *sałata*. *Sałatka* is the term used to described a salad dish usually made up of cooked vegetables and often bound in mayonnaise, such as Mixed vegetable salad, *Sałatka jarzynowa* (page 60). A *surówka*, on the other hand, is made with raw ingredients, such as sliced cucumbers or finely shredded cabbage, beets, or celeriac (celery root). So a *surówka z marchewką* is a raw carrot salad whereas a *sałatka ziemniaczana* is a cooked potato salad.
You can also think of a *surówka* as being more like a slaw, which traditionally accompanies hot meals, such as roast chicken or pork chops. *Surówki* are seasonally led, so in winter months, root vegetables, such as beets and celery root, will feature more prominently.

When salads are dressed, they are usually dressed with mayonnaise or sour cream. Lighter dressings might be made with oil, lemon juice, and plenty of chopped fresh herbs, such as dill or chives.

All of the salad recipes in this chapter can be served on their own, or as an accompaniment to a main meal. I have included a recipe for home-pickled cucumbers (page 66) too, since they are often chopped into cooked vegetable salads, and a little of the pickling juice adds good flavor to the dressing.

Left: Market stall with seasonal vegetables, fruit, and homemade pickles.

CUCUMBER, SOUR CREAM, AND DILL SALAD

MIZERIA

Mizeria was said to have been the favorite salad of Queen Bona Sforza, an Italian noblewoman who married the Polish King Sigismund I, or Zygmunt the Old, in 1518. She was homesick for Italy and was said to have brought all her Italian cooks with her to Poland to recreate the recipes that she missed. *Mizeria* derives from the Latin word for "misery." Though it doesn't have the happiest name, it is one of the best-known salads in Poland. I eat this salad with almost anything—it's a family favorite and goes equally well with cold food or as a side to a hot main dish. Traditionally, the cucumbers are peeled and sliced, but you can also use a peeler to peel long strips for a slightly different appearance.

Serves 4

1 large cucumber, peeled
   and sliced
1 tbsp sea salt
½ cup/125 ml sour cream
small bunch of fresh dill, finely
   chopped

Place the cucumber in a sieve or colander and sprinkle with the salt. Leave it to drain for 20 minutes—the salt will draw out the water from the cucumber, and it will turn slightly darker in color.

Drain well, using your hands to squeeze out any excess water, and pat dry with paper towel. Transfer the cucumber to a serving bowl. Stir in the sour cream and dill. Serve chilled.

Variation
For a lighter version, replace the sour cream with 1 teaspoon vinegar, 1 teaspoon sugar, and 1 teaspoon canola oil. Whisk these ingredients together in the serving bowl before adding the cucumber and dill.

SUMMER TOMATO SALAD

SAŁATKA POMIDOROWA

This must be made with really fresh, ripe, summer tomatoes. It is wonderful served with grilled foods alongside Cucumber, sour cream, and dill salad (page 48), or any of the raw salads or *surówki* in this chapter.

Serves 4

8 large, ripe tomatoes
sea salt and freshly ground black
  pepper
1 tsp lemon juice
1 tsp sugar
2 scallions, finely chopped
small bunch of fresh dill, chopped
¼ cup/60 ml sour cream
4 radishes, finely sliced

Slice the tomatoes and arrange them on a serving plate. Season with salt, pepper, lemon juice, and sugar. Sprinkle the scallions over the tomatoes and garnish with dill.

In a bowl, whisk the sour cream with a fork, then drizzle this over the salad. Scatter with the sliced radishes and serve.

•

AVOCADO SALAD

SAŁATKA Z AWOKADO

Avocados aren't a common Polish ingredient, but I find that the combination of avocado, cucumber, and dill works really well, and you'll often find avocado added to simple salads. You could also add some fresh tomatoes to this salad, or perhaps a chopped red pepper.

Serves 2–4

2 or 3 ripe avocados
1 large cucumber, peeled and
  finely sliced
small bunch of fresh dill,
  finely chopped
3 tbsp light olive oil
1 tbsp lemon juice
1 tsp clear honey
sea salt and freshly ground
  black pepper

Peel the avocados, remove the pits, and chop the flesh into cubes. Place in a large bowl and add the cucumber and dill.

In a separate bowl, whisk together the olive oil, lemon juice, honey, and a pinch of salt and pepper. Pour onto the avocado and cucumber, mix well, and serve immediately.

WHITE CABBAGE AND CARROT SLAW

SURÓWKA Z BIAŁEJ KAPUSTY Z MARCHEWKĄ

This is perhaps the most traditional *surówka*, or raw salad, you'll find on a Polish menu. Serve as a side dish with any main meal or try it piled into a sandwich, such as the Polish-inspired Reuben (page 107). You can also make this with drained sauerkraut. It's best if you can mix the cabbage, carrot and onion in advance, but peel and grate the apple just before adding it to the cabbage. Pictured here with Celeriac slaw with raisins (page 62).

Serves 8

½ head white cabbage, around
   1 lb 2 oz/500 g, very finely
   shredded, or 2½ cups/12 oz/
   350 g sauerkraut, drained
1 tsp sea salt
1 large carrot, grated
½ white onion, very finely chopped
freshly ground black pepper
juice of ½ lemon
1 tsp sugar
3–4 tsp vegetable oil
1 green or red apple
1 tsp chopped fresh dill or parsley

If using fresh cabbage, put it in a colander or sieve set over a bowl, sprinkle with salt, and leave to drain for 30 minutes (there is no need to salt the sauerkraut). Drain well and, using your hands, squeeze any excess water out of the cabbage.

Tip the cabbage—or sauerkraut—into a serving bowl. Add the carrot and onion. Season with a little black pepper, stir in the lemon juice, sugar, and vegetable oil, then cover and store in the fridge for up to 24 hours.

Just before serving, peel and grate the apple and add it to the cabbage. Sprinkle with the dill or parsley and serve.

GRATED BEET SALAD

SAŁATKA Z BURAKÓW

A great salad to accompany main meals, this is made with cooked beets, so it is a *salatka*, rather than a *surówka*. I pretty much always have a bowl of this in the fridge, where it can sit happily for up to two days, covered. (Pictured on page 133.)

Serves 8

4 large cooked beets, grated
½ red onion, finely chopped
sea salt and freshly ground
   black pepper
juice of ½ lemon or 1 tbsp white
   wine vinegar
1 tbsp light olive oil
2 tbsp chopped fresh dill
pinch of sugar (optional)

Mix the grated beets with the red onion, salt, and pepper. Add the lemon juice or vinegar, olive oil, and dill and mix well. Taste the salad and, if you like, sweeten it slightly with a pinch of sugar. Serve straightaway or cover and store in the fridge until ready to eat.

•

LEEK, CARROT, AND APPLE SALAD

SURÓWKA Z PORA, MARCHEWKI I JABŁKA

This is one of my Mama's favorite salads and it's quite unusual, since it makes use of fresh leeks. It's a lovely seasonal spring salad.

Serves 4

3 medium-sized leeks
   (or 6 baby leeks), cleaned
1 large carrot
1 small apple
2–3 tbsp mayonnaise
sea salt and freshly ground
   black pepper

Chop the leeks in half lengthways, then slice very finely into semi-circles. Place in a serving bowl.

Peel and grate the carrot and apple, and add to the leeks. Stir through the mayonnaise and mix well. Taste and season with a little salt and pepper. Serve.

NEW POTATO SALAD WITH POPPYSEEDS AND CHIVES

SAŁATKA Z MŁODYCH ZIEMNIAKÓW Z MAKIEM I SZCZYPIORKIEM

A Polish variation on a classic potato salad, this is a perfect salad to take along to a barbecue or picnic, or to serve as part of a buffet spread.

Serves 4

1 lb 2 oz/500 g new (or baby) potatoes
2 eggs
2 dill pickle spears, finely chopped, plus 2–3 tbsp of the pickle juice
sea salt and freshly ground black pepper
1 tbsp finely chopped fresh dill, plus a few sprigs to garnish
7 tbsp/3½ oz/100 g mayonnaise
3 tbsp sour cream
3 scallions, finely chopped
3–4 tbsp poppyseeds

Bring a large saucepan of water to a boil. Cut the potatoes in half and add to the boiling water. After 7 minutes, add the eggs and continue to cook for 8 minutes, to hard-boil them. Check the potatoes are cooked. Carefully lift out the eggs and drain the potatoes. Rinse the eggs and potatoes under cold water. Once cool enough to handle, peel the eggs and peel the potatoes—the skin should come away easily.

Chop the potatoes into small cubes and put them into a large bowl. Chop the eggs into small pieces, or mash with the back of a fork, and add to the potatoes.

Add the pickle spears and some of the pickle juice (about 1 tablespoon). Season well with salt and pepper, and stir in the chopped dill. Stir through the mayonnaise and sour cream, then leave the salad to sit for 10 minutes or so.

Just before serving, transfer to a serving bowl and sprinkle with the scallions, poppyseeds, and sprigs of dill.

The salad will keep in the fridge for up to 3 days, covered.

PICKLED CABBAGE SALAD

SURÓWKA Z CZERWONEJ I BIAŁEJ KAPUSTY

I love the purple color of this cabbage salad, flavored with caraway seeds. Think of it as a slaw, which you can take along on a picnic or serve with hot food, such as grilled meat. If you leave this salad to marinate overnight in the fridge it will wilt down a little and turn even more purple.

Serves 8

½ head white cabbage,
   around 1 lb 2 oz/500 g, ·
   very finely shredded
½ head red cabbage, around
   1 lb 2 oz/500 g, very finely
   shredded
1 tsp sea salt
1 red onion, finely chopped
1 red apple
1 tbsp white wine vinegar
1 tsp sugar
1 tbsp vegetable oil
1 tsp caraway seeds

Put the white and red cabbage in a colander or sieve set over a bowl, sprinkle the salt over the cabbage, and leave it to drain. After 30 minutes or so, squeeze any excess water out of the cabbage.

Tip the cabbage into a serving bowl. Add the red onion.

Peel and grate the apple and stir into the cabbage, along with the vinegar, sugar, oil, and caraway seeds. Serve straightaway or store in the fridge for up to 2 days.

POLISH SALAD WITH FRESH MARKET PRODUCE

SAŁATKA ZE ŚWIEŻYCH WARZYW

This is for those salad days when you come back from the market on a sunny summer's day with plenty of fresh produce. I make this almost every day during the summer months.

Serves 4

2 large round lettuce heads
½ cucumber, peeled and
    finely sliced
2 ripe tomatoes, halved
    and chopped
sea salt
juice of ½ lemon
1 tsp sugar
1 tbsp light olive oil
2 hard-boiled eggs, peeled
    and halved
4 radishes, finely sliced
2 tbsp chopped fresh chives

Wash the lettuce heads, remove the cores, drain or dry well, and break the leaves into a large salad bowl. Add the cucumber and tomatoes.

Sprinkle with salt, stir in the lemon juice, sugar, and olive oil, and mix well.

Serve with hard-boiled eggs, and sprinkle the radishes and chives over the top.

Variation
As an alternative to the lemon juice, sugar, and olive oil, stir in 2–3 tablespoons of sour cream, or heavy cream with a squeeze of lemon.

MIXED VEGETABLE SALAD
(RUSSIAN SALAD)

SAŁATKA JARZYNOWA (RUSKA SAŁATA)

I've been eating Polish mixed vegetable salad for as long as I can remember. It's one of my mom's favorite salads. It has always graced Mama's buffet table, something she is well known for whenever she hosts a party at her house.

The origins of this salad are Russian: it was created in Moscow in the 1860s by a Belgian chef called Lucien Olivier—hence it is also known as "Salad Olivier." Many Balkan and Eastern European countries have their own versions of this salad, and there are Spanish, Italian, Portuguese, and French versions, too. This was one of the recipes that I was surprised to see in Sabrina Ghayour's *Persiana*—which tells me that this salad is eaten as far afield as Iran!

In Poland, it is simply known as *sałata jarzynowa*, which means vegetable salad, and it almost always contains potatoes, peas, boiled eggs, pickled cucumbers, and mayonnaise. My Mama also sometimes adds carrots, corn, and even small white beans. All the vegetables in this salad are cooked, and leftover cooked vegetables can be used, too.

Serves 8

2–3 large potatoes,
    or 5–6 small potatoes, peeled
2 large eggs
2 large carrots, chopped into
    small cubes
⅓ cup/1¾ oz/50 g fresh or
    frozen peas
⅓ cup/1¾ oz/50 g cooked corn
⅓ cup/1¾ oz/50 g cooked
    white beans
2 dill pickle spears, finely chopped,
    plus 1 tbsp of the pickle juice
1 tsp finely chopped fresh dill
1 apple
sea salt and freshly ground
    black pepper
2–3 tbsp mayonnaise

If the potatoes are large, cut them in half; put them in a large pan of water, bring to a boil, and cook for 7 minutes. Add the eggs and continue to cook for a further 8 minutes, to hard-boil the eggs. Check the potatoes are cooked. Carefully lift out the eggs, then drain the potatoes, and set aside to cool.

Put the carrots and peas (if using fresh) in a separate pan, add water to just cover the vegetables, bring to a boil, and cook for 10 minutes, or until soft. (If using frozen peas, add them to the pan after about 7 minutes.) Drain and set aside.

Once cool enough to handle, peel the hard-boiled eggs and chop them into small pieces. Chop the potatoes into very small cubes.

Tip all the vegetables, the pickle juice, and the dill into a large bowl. Peel, core, and finely chop the apple, and add to the salad. Season with salt and pepper. Add the mayonnaise and give the vegetables a good stir until they are well coated in mayonnaise.

This salad keeps well in the fridge and tastes better if made the day before serving.

CELERIAC SLAW WITH RAISINS

SURÓWKA Z SELERA

Celeriac (or celery root) is a very underrated vegetable, but the Poles use it plentifully in raw salads. This recipe also works really well with grated carrots. It's a lovely salad in its own right, and also goes well alongside warm dishes: I like to serve it with Polish meatballs (page 118).

Serves 4

1 large celeriac (celery root), or
    4 large carrots, peeled
2 small green apples
⅓ cup/1¾ oz/50 g raisins or golden
    raisins
½ tsp sugar
2 tbsp apple juice
3 tbsp sour cream or mayonnaise
sea salt and freshly ground
    black pepper

Grate the celeriac or carrots; peel and grate the apples; if you like, you could grate them in a food processor. Tip them into a large serving bowl. Add the raisins, sugar, apple juice, and sour cream or mayonnaise, then stir well. Taste and season with salt and pepper. Serve immediately.

BUCKWHEAT AND BEET SALAD
WITH FETA, WALNUTS, AND HONEY

GRYCZANA SAŁATKA Z BURAKAMI, SEREM, ORZECHAMI I MIODEM

You can experiment with different cooked grains in this salad. I like to use buckwheat, but I have also tried this with freekeh (a Middle Eastern grain), millet, bulgur, and cracked pearl barley (*kasza jęczmienna*). You could use grilled halloumi cheese in place of the feta, or even a crumbly mild goat's cheese.

Serves 4

4 large cooked beets
⅔ cup/3½ oz/100 g buckwheat
　(*kasza gryczana*)
1¾ oz/50 g feta cheese
½ cup/1¾ oz/50 g walnut halves,
　finely chopped
2 tbsp clear honey
small bunch of fresh marjoram or
　dill, chopped

For the dressing
2 tbsp olive oil
juice of ½ lemon
sea salt and freshly ground
　black pepper

Chop the cooked beets into wedges. Set aside.

Cook the buckwheat in a large pan of salted boiling water for 15 minutes, or until tender. Drain and rinse well with cold water.

To make the dressing, mix the olive oil with the lemon juice and a pinch each of salt and pepper. Pour it over the buckwheat and stir until well coated.

Scatter the buckwheat over a large plate. Add the beets. Crumble the cheese and scatter it onto the buckwheat and beets. Scatter with the walnuts. Drizzle on the honey and garnish with marjoram or dill.

Note
If you are starting with fresh raw beets, trim the ends and put into a pan of boiling water. Cover and cook for 1 hour, or until tender. Drain and leave until cool enough to handle, then gently peel away the skin. Wear rubber gloves to avoid staining your hands.

Seasonal and raw salads | Sałatki i surówki **63**

RAINBOW BEET SALAD WITH
BUCKWHEAT AND ROASTED ASPARAGUS

TĘCZOWA SAŁATA Z BURAKAMI, KASZĄ GRYCZANĄ I PIECZONYMI SZPARAGAMI

I adore beet in all its guises: raw, roasted, cubed, grated, in soup, and in salads. This is a beautiful salad that is served warm, either on its own or as a partner to some simple grilled Polish sausage (*kiełbasa*). I love the contrast of color that the candy-striped and golden beets bring to this salad, but if you can only find one type, don't worry too much. If you would like to use pre-cooked beets, do so, but don't use pickled beets. Despite its name, buckwheat isn't related to wheat, but is related to sorrel and rhubarb. If you look very closely at buckwheat as a raw grain, you'll notice it is heart-shaped. You may find toasted or roasted buckwheat (known as kasha) as well as plain buckwheat; both work well in this salad. You can also experiment with other types of *kasza*, such as cracked pearl barley (*kasza jęczmienna*).

Serves 4

6 raw beets, preferably
    candy-striped and golden
1 lb/450 g asparagus,
    stalks trimmed
1 tsp vegetable oil
grated zest of 1 lemon
⅔ cup/3½ oz/100 g buckwheat
    (*kasza gryczana*)
1 cup/250 ml vegetable stock
1 green apple

For the dressing
2 tbsp vegetable oil, preferably
    cold-pressed organic
2 tbsp lemon juice
1 tsp honey
1 tbsp finely chopped fresh dill
sea salt and freshly ground
    black pepper

Preheat the oven to 400°F/200°C. Wash the beets and wrap each one in foil. Place on a baking sheet and bake for 1 hour. (If you are using pre-cooked beets, quarter them and roast in the oven for just 10 minutes.) Once cooked, set the beets aside to cool completely.

Arrange the asparagus on a separate baking sheet, drizzle with oil, sprinkle over the lemon zest, and roast for 10 minutes.

Meanwhile, rinse the buckwheat in cold water, drain, and put it into a saucepan with a lid. Add the vegetable stock, bring to a boil over high heat, reduce the heat, cover, and simmer gently for 8 minutes. Remove from the heat and leave to stand until all the liquid has been absorbed. Tip the buckwheat into a large bowl.

In a separate bowl, whisk together all the ingredients for the dressing.

Once the whole beets are cool enough to handle, and wearing rubber gloves to avoid pink hands, gently rub the beet skin until it comes away (I usually do this under warm running water). Cut into quarters and arrange on a plate with the asparagus and buckwheat. Finely slice the apple and scatter over the top. Drizzle the salad with the dressing, and serve.

HOMEMADE FERMENTED DILL PICKLES

DOMOWE OGÓRKI KISZONE

You will need small pickling cucumbers for this to work. Look for them at Polish stores selling fresh produce, or perhaps even a Middle Eastern grocery store; I have seen them sold as snack cucumbers. For the brine, ideally use bottled still water.

Makes 2 x 16 oz (500 ml) jars

20 small pickling cucumbers, 3–4 in/8–10 cm long
8½ cups/2 liters water
2½ tbsp table salt
2 tsp dill seeds and/or dill heads or stalks
2 bay leaves
1 tsp whole black peppercorns
5 allspice berries
2 garlic cloves, peeled
2 in/5 cm piece of fresh horseradish root, peeled (optional)

Sterilize your preserving jars (see page 207).

Soak the whole cucumbers in cold water for 1 hour. Rinse them well, pat them dry with paper towels, and leave them to dry completely.

Bring the 8½ cups/2 liters of water to a boil, add the salt, then set aside to cool until lukewarm.

Put the dill seeds, bay leaves, peppercorns, allspice berries, garlic, and horseradish, if using, into the sterilized jars and pack in the cucumbers, standing them upright.

Pour in the lukewarm brine, making sure the cucumbers are completely submerged. Close the lids and leave the cucumbers at room temperature, out of sunlight, for 2–3 days. Check them from time to time and scoop off any foam that has formed—this is simply the natural fermentation occurring.

After this time, transfer them to a cooler place, such as a cool garage or the fridge, for a week or so before eating. Make sure the cucumbers are always covered in the brine.

SEASONAL SOUPS AND MARKET-INSPIRED SIDES

ZUPY, JARZYNY I PRZYSTAWKI

It would be impossible to write a book on Polish food without including soups—in fact, they could make up a whole book of their own. Poles rarely begin a meal without soup, and you'll find everything from classic tomato or beet soups, to soups thickened with barley, as well as light, stock-based soups and consommés. When visiting Poland or a Polish restaurant, you may also notice some more unusual recipes, such as the very traditional sour rye soup served in a bread bowl, and soups made with sauerkraut and even pickled cucumbers. Mushrooms are plentiful, so there are many recipes for traditional mushroom soups.

Grains, such as barley groats (*kasze*), are often added to thicken soups and make them stretch further; for a gluten-free meal, you could add cooked rice. I have also included recipes for homemade noodles and egg-drop dumplings to add to soup.

Most soups begin with a well-flavored stock made with chicken bones or wings, or pork or beef ribs, but you can make all of these recipes with vegetable stock.

Since most of the soups in this chapter incorporate lots of fresh vegetables I suggested some seasonal sides to make the most of one bountiful trip to the market. You might even spot a kale tree!

Left: Kale tree, Bio Bazar
organic market, Warsaw.

POLISH CHICKEN SOUP

ROSÓŁ

Rosół, or chicken soup, is one of the fundamental recipes of the Polish kitchen and almost every grandmother, mother, and aunt will have perfected her own version. It's a very useful recipe to have in your repertoire, since so many other soups can be made if you begin with the method here for making a consommé, or clear stock soup. The secret is to never let it boil; simply leave the soup to gently simmer for as long as possible, ideally 2 hours, after which time you should have a perfectly clear soup. Since the rest of the ingredients are inexpensive vegetables, use the best chicken you can afford. I like to use a free-range corn-fed chicken, which imparts a beautiful golden hue to the soup. *Rosół* is traditionally served with fine egg noodles or homemade dumplings called *kluski* (page 83). I often make a batch of Homemade spelt noodles (page 81) as a variation.

Serves 8

1 whole chicken, preferably
    free-range, organic or corn-fed
8½ cups/2 liters water plus
    1 chicken or vegetable bouillon
    cube or 1 tsp bouillon powder
3 carrots
1 large white onion, halved
2 celery sticks
1 parsnip, peeled
small bunch of parsley, tied
1 tsp sea salt

To serve
2–3 tsp dried parsley or chopped
    fresh parsley
cooked egg noodles and/or *kluski*,
    dumplings (page 83)

Place the chicken in a large pan. Cover with cold water and bring to a boil over medium heat, then carefully remove the chicken and pour away the water. This first boil helps to bring out any impurities and results in a clearer stock in the long run.

Put the chicken back into the pan and pour over the 8½ cups/2 liters of water with the stock cube or bouillon powder. Add the carrots, onion (removing the dry outer peel but leaving some of the darker skin), celery, parsnip, the tied bunch of parsley, and the salt. Bring to a boil over low heat, and as soon as bubbles begin to appear, reduce the heat so that the liquid is barely simmering. Using a spoon, skim off any foam that forms on the surface of the liquid, and leave to simmer for 2 hours.

After 2 hours, strain the soup (or lift out the chicken and the vegetables). Cut the chicken into small pieces or shred the meat off the bones. Cut the carrots into small pieces.

Serve the soup with some of the chicken, the carrots, and a pinch of parsley. Add cooked noodles or dumplings.

Tip
Save the cooked onions, celery, and parsnip to add to Mama's tomato soup (page 72); the vegetables will keep in the fridge for up to 3 days.

MAMA'S TOMATO SOUP

ZUPA POMIDOROWA MOJEJ MAMY

My Mama's tomato soup was a staple in our house when we were growing up. Often, Mama made a big pan of Polish chicken soup (page 71) one day and used the leftover vegetables to make tomato soup the next, adding tomato paste, cooked tomatoes, and sour cream. If you have made the Polish chicken soup and are using the leftovers as your base, you can also add some shredded chicken for a more substantial meal. To keep this soup meat-free, use vegetable stock. If you are short on time, add a cup of tomato passata or purée in place of the cooked fresh tomatoes. Tomato soup is often served with cooked white rice; I serve it with egg vermicelli or rice noodles.

Serves 8

8½ cups/2 liters chicken stock
    (ideally follow the Polish chicken
    soup method, page 71), or
    vegetable stock
1 bay leaf
freshly ground black pepper
¼ cup/60 ml tomato paste
1 tsp vegetable oil
1 small onion, chopped
6 fresh tomatoes, chopped
1¼ cups/7 oz/200 g cooked rice
    (scant ½ cup/2½ oz/70 g dry), or
    cooked vermicelli
3 tbsp sour cream (optional)
fresh parsley leaves, to garnish

Pour the stock into a large pan and add the bay leaf and a twist of black pepper. Bring to a boil over low heat, stir in the tomato paste, and continue to simmer very gently.

Heat the oil in a frying pan, add the onion, and cook over low heat for 7–10 minutes until soft. Add the fresh tomatoes and cook for a further 5 minutes.

Transfer the onions and tomatoes to a food processor and process to a smooth purée. If you have made the Polish chicken soup and have any leftover vegetables, you can process these too for an even better flavor and a slightly thicker soup.

Tip the purée into the stock, stir, and bring back to a boil.

Add the cooked rice or vermicelli and any leftover shredded chicken, if using.

Stir in the sour cream, if using. Remove the bay leaf and serve the soup piping hot, adding a sprinkle of parsley.

TRADITIONAL BEET SOUP

BARSZCZ

Beet soup always reminds me of my *babcia,* or grandmother, because she grew beets in her garden. When she made this soup during the summer months, she added finely chopped beet stalks, plenty of fresh dill, and a handful of freshly shelled peas. In the winter she added a handful of dried mushrooms for a slightly earthier flavor, and parsley to garnish. Beet soup is eaten during the Polish Christmas Eve meal, called *Wigilia,* or vigil meal. If you are making beet soup for *Wigilia,* you should leave out the ribs, since the Christmas Eve meal is traditionally meat-free. I recommend cooking the beets separately, to retain their color, and then grating them into the soup. If the beet is added to the soup raw, the color leaks and the grated beet will appear orange. You can buy pre-cooked beet, too, but the extra step of using fresh beets is worth the effort. At a Polish grocery store, you can buy a concentrated form of beet liquid called *Barszcz Koncentrat*; add a tablespoon of this to boost the beet flavor. Otherwise, simply season well and add a good squeeze of lemon juice or red or white wine vinegar. Traditionally, beet soup is served as a consommé (on Christmas Eve, with the addition of small mushroom-filled dumplings called *uszka*). However, you can purée this soup for a slightly thicker consistency if you prefer.

Serves 8

1 lb 2 oz/500 g beef short ribs
   (leave out for a meat-free version)
2 carrots
1 white onion, halved
2 celery sticks
small bunch of parsley, tied
1 lb 2 oz/500 g raw beets,
   preferably organic, washed
a handful of dried wild mushrooms
   (optional)
sea salt and freshly ground
   black pepper
1 tbsp red wine vinegar
½ tsp sugar

Begin by making a flavorful stock. In a large pot, put the ribs, if using, carrots, onion, celery, and parsley. Cover with cold water (about 8½ cups/2 liters) and bring to a very gentle boil, using a spoon to skim off any foam that forms. Leave to simmer for 2 hours.

Put the whole, unpeeled beets into a separate pan, cover with water and a lid, and cook for 20 minutes or until the beets are soft when tested with a skewer or the tip of a knife. Drain and leave to cool.

If using dried mushrooms, put them into a cup or small bowl, pour over some freshly boiled water, and leave to soak for 5 minutes. Drain and finely chop the mushrooms. Set aside.

Once the beets are cool enough to handle, and wearing rubber gloves to avoid pink hands, carefully peel the skin away from the beets—it should come away very easily. I usually do this under warm running water.

Pour the stock through a sieve into a clean pan. Add a twist of sea salt and black pepper.

Grate the beets and add to the stock. You can grate the carrots from the stock, too. Add the chopped rehydrated mushrooms, if using. Season with salt and pepper. Heat the soup over low heat, add the vinegar and sugar, bring back to a boil, taste, and add a little more salt, pepper, vinegar, or sugar if necessary. Serve hot.

SUMMER BEET SOUP
BOTWINKA

During the summer months, try to find fresh beets with their leaves intact—if you can't find them, use a handful of fresh chives instead. Carefully remove the leaves, leaving the beets whole. Cook the beets as above. Peel and grate them into the stock. Add a handful of freshly shelled peas. Gently boil the soup for a further 5–10 minutes, or until the peas are cooked. Finely chop the beet leaves and add them to the soup. Add a little red wine vinegar and a pinch of sugar, to taste.

CHILLED BEET SOUP
CHŁODNIK

Once cooked, leave the soup to cool and then refrigerate overnight. When you are ready to serve, you can purée it in a blender if you prefer a slightly thicker consistency. Stir in (or blend in) 2–3 tablespoons of buttermilk and 2 tablespoons of full-fat plain yogurt or sour cream. Serve the soup with chopped fresh dill or chives, ½ cucumber, peeled and very finely sliced, and 4 radishes, finely sliced. A traditional accompaniment is a hard-boiled egg, cooled and peeled.

FOREST MUSHROOM SOUP

ZUPA GRZYBOWA

The Poles have an incredibly long and romantic history of mushroom hunting; it was considered to be a national pursuit, and the Polish poet and writer, Adam Mickiewicz, wrote about it in his epic poem *Pan Tadeusz*, published in Paris in 1834:

From the grove comes the whole company, carrying
   all variously, caskets,
Kerchiefs knotted at corners, or small wicker baskets
Full of mushrooms; young ladies displayed in one hand

The imposing boletus, a well-folded fan,
   In the other hand, tied like a field-flower posy,
Carried tree-and-mulch mushrooms, brown, ocher,
   and rosy.

My grandmother adored picking mushrooms and she carried the knowledge of identifying mushrooms with her throughout her life, from the forests of Poland to the forests of England and Wales, where she would look for *prawdziwki*, meaning "the true ones," or *borowiki*, porcini mushrooms, as well as other edible fungi.

Of course, you can buy all manner of wild mushrooms safely from local food markets these days, so I would probably encourage you to do that for this soup. For a meat-free version, leave the chicken out of the stock. You can serve this with cooked pearl barley (kasza) to make the traditional Polish soup, *krupnik*.

Serves 8

1 large potato, peeled
1 oz/30 g dried porcini or other
   dried wild mushrooms
1 tsp vegetable oil
1 tsp butter
1 onion, finely chopped
2 cups/7 oz/200 g fresh white
   mushrooms or mixed wild
   mushrooms, halved or quartered
juice of ½ lemon
small bunch of parsley,
   finely chopped
scant ½ cup/100 ml heavy cream
   or sour cream

For the chicken stock
1 lb 2 oz/500 g chicken wings
2 carrots
1 onion, halved
1 celery stick
small bunch of parsley
1 bay leaf, preferably fresh
sea salt and ground black pepper

To make the stock, put the ingredients and a pinch of salt and pepper into a large pot. Cover with cold water (about 8½ cups/2 liters) and gently bring to a boil, using a spoon to skim off any foam that forms. Leave to simmer for 1½ hours.

Chop the potato into small cubes, add to the stock, and cook for a further 15 minutes until the potato is soft.

Remove the chicken wings, onion, celery, and bay leaf.

Put the dried mushrooms into a cup or small bowl, pour over some boiling water, and leave to soak.

Heat the oil and butter in a large frying pan and gently fry the onion for 5 minutes, until it starts to soften. Add the fresh mushrooms and cook for 5 minutes.

Drain the rehydrated mushrooms (reserving the liquid) and chop very finely. Add to the pan with the fresh mushrooms. Squeeze in a little of the lemon juice and stir in the chopped parsley.

Tip the mushroom mixture into the stock and pour in the reserved liquid. Remove half of the soup and transfer it to a blender, process to a purée, then pour the puréed soup back into the pan. This will thicken the soup slightly. Bring back to a boil. Remove from the heat, stir in the cream, and serve.

SOUR CUCUMBER SOUP

ZUPA OGÓRKOWA

The Poles enjoy all sorts of weird and wonderful variations of sour soups. Along with this sour cucumber soup (which must be made from sour cucumbers in brine, not the sweet variety), there's also a sour sorrel soup, made in the summer with fresh sorrel leaves, and *żurek*, a soup made—like sourdough bread—with a starter, or *zakwas*. Sour, sharp, or tangy flavors often appear in soups, possibly because soups were traditionally a winter staple (often a meal in a bowl) and preserved ingredients would be added to boost flavors. This sour cucumber soup is perhaps the best one to begin with if you're new to sharp-flavored soups. There is a similar dish in *Mamushka*, by Olia Hercules, called Gherkin, beef, and barley broth, a soup that is enjoyed in Ukraine and across Eastern Europe. I suggesting beginning with a meat stock, preferably made with pork ribs, but you can leave the ribs out if you want a meat-free version. You get bonus points if you make your own fermented dill pickles (page 66) for this soup, but make sure you've left them to ferment for at least a week to get the best flavor.

Serves 8

1 lb 2 oz/500 g pork ribs (leave out for a meat-free version)
3 carrots
1 onion
2 celery sticks
1 bay leaf
2 allspice berries
sea salt and freshly ground black pepper
1 large potato, peeled
14 oz/400 g sour pickled cucumbers in brine (*ogórki kiszone*), drained
3 tbsp finely chopped fresh dill
scant ½ cup/100 ml heavy cream (optional)

Put the ribs, carrots, onion, celery, bay leaf, allspice berries, and a pinch of salt and pepper into a large pan. Cover with cold water (about 8½ cups/2 liters) and bring to a very gentle boil, using a spoon to skim off any foam that forms. Leave to simmer for 1½ hours.

Chop the potato into small cubes and add to the stock. Grate the pickled cucumbers and add to the stock. Cook for a further 15 minutes until the potato is soft. Sprinkle in the dill.

Before serving, remove the ribs and the bay leaf. Shred the meat from the bone and add the meat back into the soup. Remove the soup from heat, stir in the cream, if using, and serve.

ADDITIONS TO SOUPS

DODATEK DO ZUP

WHITE RICE

BIAŁY RYŻ

Cooked white rice can be added to Polish chicken soup (page 71) or Mama's tomato soup (page 72) in place of noodles.

1 cup/6 oz/185 g long-grain or
  basmati rice, rinsed and drained
pinch of salt
1½ cups/375 ml cold water

Tip the rice into a saucepan and add the salt and the water. Bring to a boil, then reduce the heat, cover the pan, and simmer gently, without removing the lid, for 10 minutes.

When adding pre-cooked rice to any soup, ensure that the rice is heated through thoroughly.

•

PEARL BARLEY GROATS

KASZA JĘCZMIENNA PERŁOWA

This is the best type of *kasza* to add to soups, since it is quite finely crushed, almost the size of couscous. Whole pearl barley works well, too, particularly with the Forest mushroom soup (page 76), although it takes a lot longer to cook.

1¼ cups/9 oz/250 g crushed
  pearl barley

Rinse the barley in cold water. Drain, tip into a saucepan, and add enough cold water to cover the barley. Bring to a boil, then reduce the heat and simmer, uncovered, for 10–15 minutes.

Whole pearl barley will need to be cooked for anything from 45 minutes to 1¼ hours, until tender, then drained—and rinsed, if it is not added straight into the soup.

HOMEMADE SPELT NOODLES
DOMOWY MAKARON ORKISZOWY

These homemade noodles go well with Polish chicken soup (page 71). You can also buy good-quality spelt noodles. Spelt, *orkisz* in Polish, is an ancient grain, said to be one of the earliest domesticated grains and nutritionally better for you than modern wheat, though it is not gluten free. You can make the dough in a stand mixer with a knead function if you have one. I like to make tagliatelle-width noodles, using a pasta machine. If you don't have a pasta machine, make sure you roll your dough as thinly as possible before cutting.

2½ cups/10½ oz/300 g spelt flour, plus extra for dusting
1 tsp salt, plus extra for the noodles
3 eggs
1 tbsp light olive oil

Tip the flour and salt onto your work surface or a board. Make a well in the center. Crack in the eggs and pour in the olive oil. Using a knife, gently bring the flour and eggs together until a ball starts to form. You may need to add a tablespoon of water to bring it together.

Dust your work surface with flour. Knead the dough, pushing it away from you with the palm of your hand and then bringing it back, for around 5 minutes, until the dough pushes back up if you poke it. Form the dough into a ball, wrap in plastic wrap, and leave to rest at room temperature for 30 minutes.

Cut the dough into four pieces. Working with one piece at a time, roll the dough as thinly as possible (or put it through a pasta machine—start at 6, the widest setting, and keep rolling it through and lowering the setting until you get to 1). Cut it into ½ in/1 cm strips. Repeat until all the dough is used.

To cook the noodles, bring a large pan of water to a boil. Add a large pinch of salt and the noodles, and cook for 5 minutes, or until the noodles float to the top of the boiling water. Drain and serve, or add to soup.

Continued_

_Continued

EGG DROP DUMPLINGS OR TEASPOON DUMPLINGS
KLUSKI KŁADZIONE ŁYŻKĄ

These are classic Polish egg dumplings that are simple to make and go wonderfully well with Polish chicken soup (page 71) or any light broth. My *babcia* (grandmother) loved to make these for me when I was a child, and now I love making them with my own children. Until you are skilled at making these like a *babcia*, I recommend that you cook them by dropping them into boiling water, rather than directly into your soup. The method I have given here is for "teaspoon" *kluski*, but you can also pour the batter through a colander over the pan, which produces thin, soft noodles, similar to spätzle, or through a funnel, which will create different shapes.

2 eggs
½ cup/2 oz/60 g all-purpose
  flour
pinch of sea salt

Crack the eggs into a large bowl and whisk them with a fork. Add the flour and salt, and mix everything together until you have a thick, but just pourable, batter.

Bring a saucepan of water to a boil (or your pan of chicken soup if you are feeling brave) and taking a teaspoonful of batter at a time, carefully drop the batter into the boiling liquid. Boil for a minute or so, until the dumplings rise to the top.

APPLE MASHED POTATOES

TŁUCZONE ZIEMNIAKI Z JABŁKAMI

At the end of our backyard we have a huge apple tree, so we're always looking for ways to use the fruit. Apples are Poland's largest export and the Poles are very fond of apple recipes. This apple mash goes really well with Polish meatballs (page 118), pork dishes, fried liver and onions, or with roasted duck.

Serves 4

1 lb 12 oz/800 g potatoes, peeled
1 tsp vegetable oil
2 tsp butter
½ white onion, finely chopped
2 large apples, peeled and cubed
pinch of salt

Cut the potatoes into quarters and place in a large pan of water. Bring to a boil, reduce the heat, and simmer gently for 10–15 minutes, or until the potatoes are cooked.

Meanwhile, heat the oil and half the butter in a frying pan, add the onion, and fry gently for 10 minutes until soft and translucent.

Add the apples and fry for 5 minutes. Add 2 tablespoons of water to the pan to prevent the mixture from getting too dry, then continue to cook until the apples are soft.

Drain the potatoes, put them back into their pan, and mash until smooth—or push them through a potato ricer. Stir in the cooked apples and add the remaining butter and the salt. Serve hot.

RED CABBAGE WITH CARAWAY SEEDS

CZERWONA KAPUSTA Z KMINKIEM

I couldn't write a Polish recipe book without sneaking in a few cabbage recipes, and I hope they will convince you that cabbage is a great vehicle for flavor, as well as being very inexpensive. This is a lovely side dish, flavored with caraway, which is a typical Polish flavor. If you're not keen on caraway, try fennel seeds instead. I don't think we eat enough red cabbage; it's very underrated and usually only appears around the holidays. Try this with any of the pork dishes in this book, or even the roast duck— it works really well. If you like, you can purée this cabbage (you can do the same with beets) for an alternative and more modern texture. Pictured here with White cabbage with bacon (page 88).

Serves 8

1 head red cabbage
2 tsp vegetable oil
1 tsp butter
1 red onion, finely diced
2 red apples, peeled and sliced
  or chopped
2 tsp caraway seeds, lightly bashed
2 tbsp red wine vinegar
1 tsp honey
½ cup/125 ml vegetable stock
sea salt and freshly ground
  black pepper

Cut the cabbage in half and remove the core. Slice the cabbage, then roughly chop into smaller pieces.

In a large, heavy-based pan or Dutch oven, heat the oil and butter, add the onion, apples, and caraway seeds, and cook over low heat for 10 minutes until softened.

Add the cabbage, vinegar, honey, and stock. Season, stir well, and simmer for 30 minutes until the cabbage is tender. Serve hot.

Tip
If puréeing, leave the mixture to cool slightly, then transfer to a high-powered blender and blend to a purée.

WHITE CABBAGE WITH BACON

KAPUSTA Z BOCZKIEM

You can try this recipe with any type of cabbage that you like. The Poles would use a large white cabbage, but savoy works well, as does sweetheart (also known as hispi or pointed cabbage). You could make this dish suitable for vegetarians by leaving out the bacon. I use the Polish bacon called *boczek*, but pancetta would work equally well (pictured on page 87).

Serves 6

1 large white cabbage
1 tsp vegetable oil
1 tsp butter
1 large white onion, finely chopped
5½ oz/150 g Polish bacon or
   pancetta, chopped
2 tbsp tomato paste
½ cup/125 ml vegetable stock
1 tsp sugar or honey
sea salt and freshly ground
   black pepper
2 tsp chopped fresh dill, to serve

Remove any tough outer leaves from the cabbage, cut it in half, and remove the core, and then finely chop.

In a large, heavy-based pan or Dutch oven, heat the oil and butter, add the onion, and fry for 5 minutes until it starts to soften. Add the bacon and cook for a further 5 minutes, until it starts to turn a little crispy.

Tip in the cabbage and stir well to mix it with the onion and bacon. Stir in the tomato paste, stock, and the sugar or honey. Season with salt and pepper, and leave to simmer gently for 30 minutes. To serve, sprinkle with fresh dill.

NEW POTATOES WITH BUTTER AND DILL

MŁODE ZIEMNIAKI Z MASŁEM I KOPERKIEM

There's only one way to eat freshly boiled young potatoes Polish-style, and that's with plenty of sea salt, butter, and fresh dill.

1 lb/450 g new or baby potatoes, rinsed
small bunch of fresh dill, chopped
1 tsp sea salt
2 tbsp butter

Put the potatoes into a large saucepan and cover with cold water. Bring to a boil, then reduce the heat and simmer for 10–12 minutes, until the potatoes are tender when pierced with a knife.

Drain the potatoes, then return them to the pan. Sprinkle with dill and sea salt, and add the butter. Cover the pan with a lid and shake well so that the butter melts and the potatoes are covered in dill. Transfer to a bowl and serve.

ASPARAGUS À LA POLONAISE

SZPARAGI PO POLSKU

I love the term "à la Polonaise," a French term meaning "in the Polish manner," because it conjures up a bygone era of French cooks in the 19th century being influenced by the Polish way of cooking, thanks to a wave of émigrés settling in Paris. The term refers to a garnish for cooked vegetables: a topping of buttery breadcrumbs, sometimes with chopped hard-boiled egg. You can use this topping for all manner of market vegetables, such as Brussels sprouts, cabbage, cauliflower, green beans, or leeks. You could also use it as a topping for meat or fish: roasted cod works well. I have modernized this recipe slightly by using sourdough bread morsels and adding a softly poached egg. Serve this for lunch or supper, with brunch, or with the fish recipes on pages 147 and 148.

Serves 2

about 1 lb/450 g fresh asparagus,
    stalks trimmed
¼ cup/1¾ oz/50 g butter
1 tbsp vegetable oil
2 slices of sourdough bread,
    torn into small pieces or
    chopped into cubes
2 eggs
2 tsp white wine vinegar
grated zest of ½ lemon
sea salt
1 tsp chopped fresh dill

Plunge the asparagus into a large pan of boiling water. Cook for 5 minutes. Drain and set aside.

Heat the butter and oil in a large frying pan. Add the bread pieces, tossing until well coated and frying for 3–4 minutes, until golden and crisp.

To poach the eggs, bring a large wide pan of water to a boil. Add the vinegar. Stir the boiling water with a spoon to create a whirlpool effect. One by one, crack the eggs into the center of the whirlpool. Cook over low heat for 3 minutes, until the egg whites are firm but the yolks are still soft. Carefully remove the eggs with a slotted spoon and drain on paper towels.

Place the cooked asparagus on two plates. Top with the buttery bread cubes and a poached eggs. Sprinkle with the lemon zest, sea salt, and dill.

CARROTS WITH HONEY AND STAR ANISE

MARCHEWKA Z MIODEM I ANYŻEM

The classic Polish way of cooking carrots is to boil them in very little water, just enough to cover them, adding butter and a little sugar. You have to watch them carefully, but as the water, butter, and sugar cook down into a glaze, you'll be left with very tasty, tender carrots. Here, I've used honey instead of sugar and I have also added the more unusual flavoring of star anise—a trick I picked up from chef Marek Kropielnicki in Warsaw. You could try adding caraway seeds in place of the star anise.

Serves 4

8 carrots
1 tbsp butter
1 tsp honey
1 star anise (or 1 tsp caraway
　seeds, lightly bashed)
2 tsp chopped flat-leaf parsley,
　to garnish (optional)

Peel the carrots, halve or quarter them lengthways, and put them into a wide saucepan. Add the butter, honey, and star anise. Add cold water to just cover the carrots. Bring to a boil, then reduce the heat to very low and cook for 15 minutes.

Check that the water hasn't boiled dry—there should be some liquid around the carrots all the time. If the carrots are still a little hard, continue cooking for a further 5 minutes, or until soft.

You won't need to drain the carrots, since there should be only a little liquid left by the time they are soft. Serve hot, with a sprinkle of parsley, if using.

Tip
You can purée these carrots using a handheld immersion blender—just remove the star anise first. Add an extra tablespoon or two of water, if needed.

LIGHT BITES AND STREET FOOD

ZAKĄSKI I PRZEKĄSKI

The concept of *zakąski*, "small bites," comes from the Russian *zakuski*, which is a tradition dating back to the 19th century. Imagine a gilded ballroom, like something from Tolstoy's *War and Peace*, lined with large tables laden with snacks to keep guests happy—the guests being the landed gentry, living on large estates, often entertaining their peers. During the same period, Anton Chekhov wrote: "You must make sure that your mind dwells on nothing but the wineglass and the appetizer."

In her classic Russian cookbook *Please to the Table*, Anya von Bremzen introduces *zakuski* to "accompany chilled shots of vodka with a glittering array of little dishes… A most inviting way to begin a meal." However, the origin of *zakuski* almost certainly goes back to the Scandinavian smorgasbord, "an hypothesis made more plausible by the fact that the great pre-Christian Russian rulers, such as Rurik, were of Scandinavian stock," says Anya.

The practice of eating *zakąski* in Poland today may be a little different in style to Tolstoy's Russia, but the concept of greeting a guest with a hot or cold *hors d'oeuvre* continues to have a special place in Polish life. At home, *zakąski* may be served as canapés, or as a buffet before a main meal, or even as the main event itself—my Mama's buffets are legendary. The small bites are usually whatever the hosts feel most comfortable preparing. For a Polish-style buffet, set out a selection of the small bites within this chapter, some Polish charcuterie or *wędliny*, pickles, and a selection of salads from Chapter 2. If you are catering for a large number of guests, you could follow the hot and cold small bites with a more substantial meal of Meatballs with mushroom sauce (page 118) and a big pan of *Bigos* (pages 111 or 125).

In modern Poland, the concept of small bites is becoming more and more trendy within cocktail bars and gastropubs. If you join a city vodka tour, you'll almost certainly be introduced to a whole new world of Polish *tapas*. Equally fun is the concept of street food—snacks that you might grab quickly, known as *przekąski*. Food trucks are a rapidly growing trend across cities in Poland. I often enjoy recreating street-food recipes for friends, or when hosting a barbecue in sunny weather.

Left: Pastry rolls, with sauerkraut and mushrooms, Old Town, Warsaw.

PASTRY ROLLS WITH SAUERKRAUT AND MUSHROOMS

PASZTECIKI Z KISZONĄ KAPUSTĄ I Z GRZYBAMI

I had these little vegan pastry rolls on a cold November day at a food market near the old town in Warsaw. They make a great alternative to a traditional sausage roll and they go well with Traditional beet soup (page 74); they could be served at the *Wigilia* table on Christmas Eve. To ensure these pastry rolls are vegan, make sure that you buy butter-free puff pastry (rather than all-butter).

Makes 16

1 oz/30 g dried porcini or other
   dried wild mushrooms
1½ tbsp vegetable oil
1 white onion, finely chopped
2½ cups/12 oz/350 g sauerkraut,
   preferably organic, rinsed,
   drained, and finely chopped
5½ oz/150 g fresh wild or
   cultivated mushrooms, finely
   chopped
½ cup/125 ml vegetable stock
sea salt and freshly ground
   black pepper
2 rectangular sheets (1 lb 9 oz/
   700 g) ready-rolled puff pastry
⅔ cup/150 ml almond milk

Preheat the oven to 350°F/180°C. Put the dried mushrooms into a cup or small bowl, pour over some freshly boiled water, and leave to soak.

Heat the oil in a large frying pan, add the onion, and gently fry for 10–15 minutes until soft and golden.

Add the sauerkraut to the frying pan and cook for 5 minutes. Add the chopped fresh mushrooms. Drain the soaked mushrooms, finely chop, and add them to the sauerkraut. Pour in the stock and season with salt and pepper. Transfer to a baking dish, cover with foil, and bake for 1 hour.

Remove the sauerkraut mixture from the oven, pour off any liquid, and set aside until cool enough to handle. Increase the oven temperature to 400°F/200°C.

Line two large baking sheets with parchment paper.

Unroll the pastry on your work surface and cut each sheet in half lengthways so that you have four pieces. Using a teaspoon, carefully spoon the sauerkraut mixture along the middle of each length of pastry.

Brush the long edges of the pastry with almond milk. Fold the pastry over the filling and gently press the edges together to seal. Using a sharp knife, cut each long roll into four smaller pieces. Transfer the pastry rolls onto the lined baking sheets, brush the tops with almond milk, and bake for 25 minutes, or until the pastry is golden and crisp. Serve warm.

HERRINGS IN COLD-PRESSED LINSEED OIL

ŚLEDZIE W OLEJU LNIANYM

You can't really separate the Pole from the herring, it is a very loyal partnership. Herrings are plentiful in the Baltic Sea (the only species in the Baltic not threatened by overfishing are herring, sprat, and mackerel) and very high in healthy omega-3 fats. My grandmother adored them and used to bring fresh herrings home from the market and salt them herself in a large bucket. These days, you can find lots of different types of herring: salted, or preserved in brine, oil, or vinegar. In Poland, the best herrings you can buy are called *matias*, *matjes*, or *matiasy*. They are young herring fillets, which often have a pink tinge to them. This is my Mama's method for preparing herrings, which transforms a plain, salty thing into something flavorsome and versatile. Whereas Poles will usually use sunflower or vegetable oil, I have suggested a cold-pressed linseed (flaxseed) oil (*olej lniany*), which offers a double hit of omega 3. Herrings almost always appear on the table whenever my Mama hosts a party. Herrings, served with rye bread, are often enjoyed with a small glass of vodka. You will need a 1-quart (1-liter) jar, such as a clip-top preserving jar.

Makes 4 cups/1 liter
12 herring fillets (salted, or in brine or oil)
2 white onions, finely sliced
2 bay leaves, preferably fresh
1 tsp whole black peppercorns
generous ¾ cup/200 ml cold-pressed, organic linseed (flaxseed) oil

If the herrings are salted, you will need to soak them in cold water for 24 hours, changing the water several times. Drain the herrings and dry them on paper towels. If you are using herrings in brine or oil, drain them in a colander. Chop the herrings into 2 in/5 cm pieces.

Put the onions into a large bowl. Pour over some freshly boiled water, leave for 5 minutes, then drain the water.

Sterilize a 1-quart (1-liter) jar. Layer the onions, herrings, bay leaves, and peppercorns in the jar.

Pour in the oil until the herrings are completely covered. Seal with a tight-fitting lid.

These herrings will be ready to eat in a day or two, and will keep in the fridge (as long as they are immersed in oil) for a month.

Eat them as they are, on rye bread, or with one of the following toppings (see overleaf).

Continued_

_Continued

WITH GREEN APPLE AND HONEY

herrings, as on previous page
1 large green apple, sliced
½ bulb fennel, finely shredded (optional)
small bunch of fresh dill, chopped
juice of ½ lemon
1 tbsp clear honey
2 tbsp cold-pressed, organic linseed (flaxseed) oil

Remove the herrings from the oil and arrange them on a plate. Top with sliced apple, shredded fennel, if using, and sprigs of dill. Drizzle with lemon juice, honey, and linseed oil. Serve with rye bread.

Tip
This works really well with fresh herring fillets, too. Fry the herring fillets skin-side down. Pan-fry or griddle the fennel bulb. Top with green apple slices, dill, a drizzle of lemon juice, honey, and linseed oil.

WITH SOUR CREAM

herrings, as on previous page
1 small apple, peeled and cubed
1 small red onion, finely sliced
scant ½ cup/100 ml sour cream
1 tsp lemon juice
1 tsp sugar
small bunch of fresh dill, chopped

Remove the herrings from the oil and arrange them on a plate. Scatter the apple and red onion over the top.

In a bowl, whisk the sour cream, lemon juice, and sugar. Pour this sauce over the herrings. Scatter with the dill and serve with rye bread.

WITH RED ONION AND CHIVES

herrings, as on previous page
1 small red onion, very finely sliced
2 tsp chopped fresh chives
2 tbsp cold-pressed, organic linseed (flaxseed) oil

Remove the herrings from the oil and arrange them on a plate. Sprinkle over the red onion and chives, and drizzle with linseed oil. Serve with rye bread.

STEAK TARTARE

TATAR

The best tartare dish I ever tasted was very recently, in Warsaw. It was made by a chef called Marek Kropielnicki, who, like me, grew up in Manchester as a second-generation Pole. He has now married and made Warsaw his home. Marek's tartare was made with wild venison, from a female roe deer that he had hunted himself. The tartare was served on a bed of moss gathered from the Mazury region, with clouds of dry ice floating on the table for added effect. It was quite spectacular. Marek's advice was, of course, to use the best beef or venison that you can find—grass-fed, organic is best. Most people chop the meat finely, but Marek takes a knife and scrapes the fillet so that you get an incredibly fine, almost mousse-like texture, rather than small chunks. My friends Bożena and Mariola, also "Manchester Poles," remember their father, Pan Andrzej, making his tartare this way, too. His secret was to add a drop of oil from a can of sardines or anchovies. Marek's secret ingredient from modern-day Warsaw is lovage oil; he also adds chopped pickled mushrooms and cornichons. Lovage can be grown very easily in the garden, and the leaves add a wonderful, deep, savory note to this oil. You can use this method to make other herb oils, for example using wild garlic leaves or chives: these will be too strong for the steak tartare, but would be delicious drizzled over *Kaszotto* (page 121) or grilled meat.

Serves 2

9 oz/250 g organic, grass-fed beef fillet or venison fillet
2 cornichons, finely chopped
1 tbsp pickled mushrooms, drained
1 red onion or shallot, very finely chopped
½ tsp nigella seeds
sea salt and freshly ground black pepper
2 tsp lovage oil (see below), or oil from a can of anchovy fillets, or cold-pressed avocado oil
1 tsp boiled, cooled water
2 fresh quail's eggs

For the lovage oil (optional)
1 oz/30 g (a small handful) fresh lovage leaves, washed and dried
⅓ cup/80 ml grapeseed or vegetable oil

Prepare the steak immediately before serving it, otherwise the meat will begin to oxidize and discolor.

Very finely chop the steak into tiny cubes, or mince it, or scrape it with the edge of a knife along the fillet. Place it in a bowl. Add the cornichons, mushrooms, and the red onion or shallot. Add the nigella seeds and season well with salt and pepper. Add the oil and the boiled, cooled water. Stir with a fork to combine well.

To serve, place a chef's ring on each plate. Spoon equal quantities of the steak into the rings, then remove the rings.

Pour hot water over the quail's eggs to remove any bacteria on the outside of the shell. Crack the eggs, separate the yolks from the whites and serve the yolk next to the steak tartare.

To make your own lovage oil
Put the lovage leaves into a high-powered blender, pour in the oil, and process for 10 minutes. The oil will heat up slightly due to the friction of the blade.

Place a piece of sterile gauze in a sieve over a bowl (or use a coffee filter paper) and pour the liquid into the sieve. Leave to drip through overnight. The result should be a clear, green oil. Transfer the oil to a plastic bottle and use on salads, over herrings, or in this steak tartare. Use within 2–3 days.

POTATO BLINIS WITH SMOKED SALMON AND SOUR CREAM

BLINY KARTOFLANE Z KWAŚNĄ ŚMIETANĄ I ŁOSOSIEM

These blinis are made in much the same way as *placki*, large potato pancakes (page 128). The blinis also go well with the herring recipes in this chapter.

Makes about 30–32 small pancakes

4 large baking potatoes (about
    1 lb 7 oz/650 g), peeled
1 banana shallot
1 egg, beaten
2 tbsp all-purpose flour
sea salt and freshly ground
    black pepper
3 tbsp vegetable oil

To serve
6 tbsp/90 ml sour cream
a few slices of smoked salmon
a few sprigs of fresh dill

Using the coarse side of a cheese grater, grate the potatoes and place them in a sieve or colander set over a bowl. Leave for about 5 minutes to allow excess liquid to drain, then use the back of a spoon or your hands to squeeze the potatoes to remove most of the liquid.

Grate the shallot into a large bowl. Add the potatoes, beaten egg, and flour. Season with salt and pepper, then stir everything together—the mixture should be quite thick.

Heat the oil in a frying pan over medium heat. Drop tablespoonfuls of the mixture into the hot oil and flatten with a spatula. Fry for 1–2 minutes on each side, turning once, until golden brown. Transfer the blinis to a board lined with a paper towel and leave to cool slightly.

To serve, top each blini with ½ teaspoon of sour cream, a small piece of smoked salmon, and some dill.

FOREST MUSHROOMS WITH THYME CREAM ON SOURDOUGH

GRZYBY W ŚMIETANIE NA CHLEBIE

This is really a simple "on toast" recipe and it's my favorite way of serving wild mushrooms after a day of *grzybobranie*, or mushroom picking. You can use any wild mushrooms or use cultivated mushrooms, *pieczarki*, instead. The sort of mushrooms you'll likely find in Poland include *prawdziwki* (porcini), *podgrzybki* (bay bolete), *maślaki* (boletus), or *kurki* (chanterelle). You can also serve this as hors d'oeuvres or small bites—simply slice the sourdough into quarters after toasting.

Serves 2

generous ¾ cup/200 ml heavy cream
2 sprigs of fresh thyme
1 tsp butter
1 tsp vegetable oil
1 white onion, finely chopped
14 oz/400 g mixed wild mushrooms, cleaned and chopped
sea salt and freshly ground black pepper
2 slices of sourdough bread, to serve
fresh marjoram leaves or chopped parsley, to serve

Pour the cream into a small saucepan, add the thyme sprigs, and bring the cream to a gentle boil. Switch off the heat after 5 minutes and leave the cream to stand.

Heat the butter and oil in a frying pan, add the onion, and cook over very gentle heat for 10 minutes.

Add the mushrooms to the pan, season well with salt and pepper, and fry gently for 15 minutes.

Remove the thyme from the cream. Pour the cream over the mushrooms and stir.

Toast the bread or grill in a grill pan. Spoon the mushrooms over the toast, and scatter over some marjoram or parsley. Serve.

REN'S REUBEN

KANAPKA REUBENA Z KIEŁBASĄ

The Reuben sandwich is a classic American hot sandwich made with finely sliced corned beef, cheese, sauerkraut, and Thousand Island dressing. This is my American Polonia-inspired version, made with smoked Polish sausage. It's really a tribute to my sister Basia and her family, who live in the US and are therefore the American Polonia contingent in our family. The "Polish Reuben" is definitely something you'd find at a large Polish food festival, perhaps somewhere like Chicago, where there are almost as many Poles as there are in Warsaw. When visiting my sister, I became quite partial to the Seattle Dog, or "Polish Dog," made on street carts with grilled Polish sausage, served in a soft bun with caramelized onions, cabbage, and cream cheese—I would go back there tomorrow for one of those! The dressing here is made with horseradish and mayonnaise, but feel free to use Thousand Island if you prefer. I like to make mini Polish Reubens, using small sub rolls, for parties and gatherings.

Serves 2

½ ring Polish sausage, such
    as *wiejska*
4 slices of sourdough rye bread,
    or 2 rolls or buns
2 slices of cheese
1½ cups/7 oz/200 g sauerkraut,
    well drained
¼ cup/1¾ oz/50 g butter, softened

For the dressing
⅔ cup/150 ml sour cream or
    mayonnaise
2 tbsp creamy horseradish sauce
    (or ketchup)
sea salt and freshly ground
    black pepper

Mix the ingredients for the dressing together in a small bowl and set aside.

Heat a frying pan and gently fry the sausage until it starts to get some color and is warmed through. Slice the sausage into thin diagonal slices.

If using rolls or buns, split them and toast them, cut-side down.

Spread two slices of bread (or two bun halves) with the dressing. Divide the sausage between the bread or buns, place a slice of cheese on each, and top with sauerkraut. Top with the slices of bread (or bun halves). Butter the top and bottom slices. Reheat the frying pan, add the sandwiches and place over a medium–high heat until lightly toasted on both sides. (You can also use a sandwich press or a grill pan.) Slice and serve straight away.

Seattle "Polish Dog"
For this version, fry some sliced onions, along with ¼ head shredded white cabbage until golden. Spread the buns with cream cheese. Grill the sausage and top with the onion and cabbage mixture and a squeeze of mayonnaise or mustard.

POLISH FLATBREADS WITH ZUCCHINI, RED CABBAGE, AND ARUGULA

PODPŁOMYK Z CUKINIĄ, CZERWONĄ KAPUSTĄ I RUKOLĄ

A *podpłomyk* is a type of Polish flatbread, similar to a tortilla; it's a type of bread that most Polish people might remember their grandmother making, but you can now find *podpłomyk* at Polish food festivals and street food markets. Here's the way I like to eat them, but they are equally good straight from the pan, just as they are. Look out too for *zapiekanki*, a sort of baguette-pizza, topped with all kinds of ingredients, my favorite being tomato, mushrooms, and cheese, garnished with fresh chives.

Makes 6

4 cups/1 lb 2 oz/500 g white, wholewheat, or rye flour (or a blend), plus extra for dusting
1 cup/250 ml water
pinch of salt
2 tsp cold-pressed canola oil, plus extra for drizzling
1 tsp honey
2 zucchini, peeled into strips
½ head red cabbage, finely shredded
a handful of arugula leaves

Sift the flour into a bowl and stir in the water, salt, 1 teaspoon of the oil, and the honey. Bring the mixture together by hand to create a ball of dough—you can also do this in a food processor.

Tip the dough out onto a lightly floured surface and knead for 5 minutes, until smooth and elastic. Wrap in plastic wrap and leave to rest for 10 minutes.

Divide the dough into six pieces and cover with a damp dish towel. Sprinkle a little flour onto your work surface and roll out each piece of dough into a circle about ¼ in/5 mm thick.

Heat a large frying pan and place one flatbread at a time into the dry pan over low heat. Cook for 1–2 minutes on each side, taking care not to burn the bread.

For the topping, heat a griddle pan and brush with the remaining 1 teaspoon of oil. Place the zucchini pieces flat onto the pan and cook for 1–2 minutes on each side, until nicely charred. Top the flatbreads with the chargrilled zucchini strips, scatter with the red cabbage and arugula leaves, and serve drizzled with canola oil.

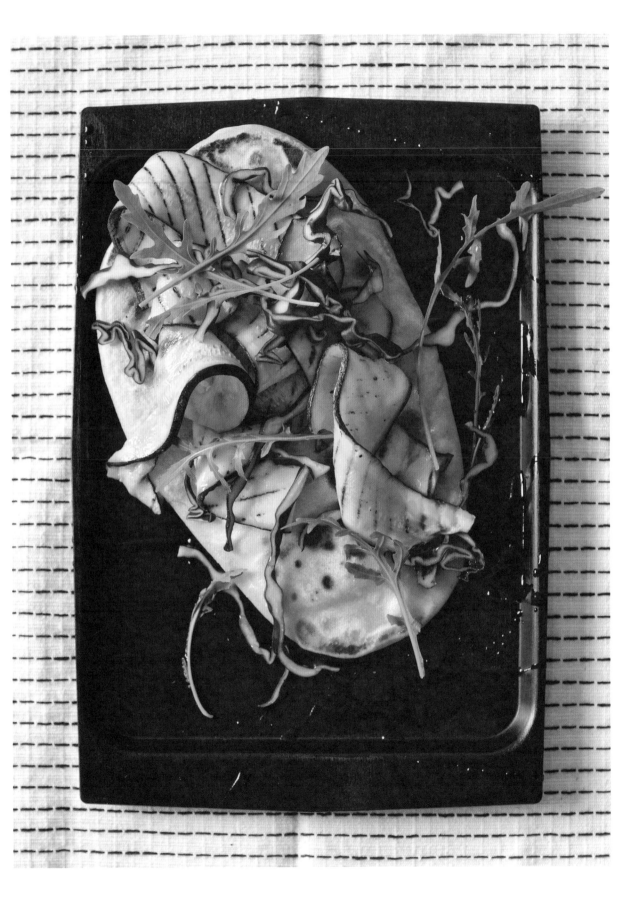

"FEED A CROWD" HUNTER'S STEW

BIGOS MAMY

In Poland, *bigos* was traditionally made in manor houses with many types of leftover meat—pork, beef, lamb, game, Polish sausage—as well as cabbage; it was given to the men to take with them when they went hunting, hence it is often referred to as "hunter's stew." During the hunt it would be heated up in a huge pot over a fire and eaten with bread. It is now known as Poland's national dish and there are many versions. The flavor improves when it is reheated—some Polish cooks spend three days cooking their *bigos*! I once fed 150 food bloggers with *bigos*, based on Mama's recipe. I was delighted at how much it was enjoyed—there was not a single spoonful left. I also had some flavorful *bigos* recently at a winter food market in Warsaw. Served with rye bread, it was utterly delicious, and set me up for a visit to the Royal Castle in the Old Town.

Serves 8–12

1¾ oz/50 g dried porcini
 mushrooms
6 cups/2 lb/900 g sauerkraut
 (I use 2 x 15 oz/410g jars of
 organic, raw, fresh sauerkraut)
3 tbsp vegetable oil
1 tsp butter
2 large onions, chopped
1 lb 2 oz/500 g pork belly or
 pork shoulder, chopped into
 small cubes
4 *kabanosy* (thin, smoked Polish
 sausages), chopped into ½ in/
 1 cm pieces
7 oz/200 g (½ ring) *kiełbasa*, Polish
 sausage, chopped into cubes
4 allspice berries
2 prunes or 1 tbsp *powidła*,
 Polish plum butter
2 bay leaves, preferably fresh
6 cups/1.5 liters chicken stock
sea salt and freshly ground
 black pepper
1 cup/3½ oz/100 g fresh white
 mushrooms, chopped
½ head white cabbage,
 finely shredded
rye bread, to serve

Preheat the oven to 400°F/200°C. Put the dried porcini into a cup or small bowl, pour over some freshly boiled water, and leave to soak.

Drain the sauerkraut into a sieve. If you would prefer a slightly less sour flavor, rinse the sauerkraut with cold water and then drain it. If you like sour, then simply squeeze out the liquid using your hands. Set to one side.

Heat 2 tablespoons of the oil and the butter in a large ovenproof pot or Dutch oven and add the onions. Cook over very low heat for 10–15 minutes, until the onions are very soft and lightly golden.

Add the pork to the pan and cook over low heat for about 10 minutes, allowing it to brown slowly while the fat is released.

Add the sausages to the pan and stir. Tip in the sauerkraut. Drain the porcini mushrooms (reserving the liquid), roughly chop, and add them to the pan. Add the allspice berries, prunes or *powidła*, and bay leaves, and pour in the reserved mushroom soaking liquid, being careful not to add any of the grit at the bottom of the cup. Pour in the stock and season well with salt and pepper. Cover with a lid or foil and cook in the oven for 1½ hours; after the first 15 minutes turn the oven down to 350°F/180°C. Alternatively, you can cook your *bigos*, covered, over low heat on the stovetop.

Towards the end of the cooking time, fry the fresh mushrooms in a separate pan with 1 tablespoon of oil. Add to the sauerkraut, along with the fresh cabbage, stir well, and bake for a further 1 hour, covered.

If there is a lot of liquid left in the *bigos*, put the pan over medium heat and simmer, uncovered, for around 10 minutes, or until some of the liquid evaporates. The *bigos* is best eaten the day after cooking, after being thoroughly reheated. Serve with rye bread.

POLISH OPEN SANDWICHES

KANAPKI

Kanapki, from the French word *canapé*, are a staple in Poland, very similar to Scandinavian open sandwiches and simple to make. The Poles eat *kanapki* for breakfast, or sometimes for their second breakfast, *drugie śniadanie*. *Kanapki* can also form part of a brunch or buffet table, or may be eaten as a snack later in the day with a little glass of something in hand. You can buy most of the toppings from the deli counter. Leftover cold cuts, such as roast beef, work well, too. You can either make these sandwiches for your guests, or cut some bread and serve everything on the table so that your guests can help themselves.

Serves 4–6

1 loaf of bread, preferably rye
  or sourdough, sliced
butter, softened
9 oz/250 g cheese, such as
  Edam, sliced
5½ oz/150 g *twaróg*, farmer's
  cheese, or cream cheese
5½ oz/150 g smoked salmon,
  sliced
9 oz/250 g Polish roasted or cured
  ham or pork loin, such as *wiejska*
  or *sopocka*, sliced
9 oz/250 g cured or smoked Polish
  sausage, sliced
5½ oz/150 g *pasztet* or pâté,
  preferably liver pâté or chicken
  liver pâté
sea salt and freshly ground
  black pepper

Suggested garnishes
2–3 hard-boiled eggs, sliced
1 bunch of radishes, finely sliced
4 tomatoes, finely sliced
½ fresh cucumber or 4 dill pickles,
  finely sliced
2 tbsp fresh dill, marjoram, or
  watercress, leaves picked

Butter each slice of bread and lay the slices in a single layer on a large plate or board. I usually top a quarter of the bread with cheese slices, a quarter with soft cheese and smoked salmon, and the remaining half with a selection of deli meats and pâté.

Season with salt and pepper and then top with a selection of the garnishes. It looks pretty if each sandwich has a slice of egg, radish, tomato, and cucumber on top. Once assembled, scatter the green herbs over the sandwiches and serve.

GRILLED POLISH CHARCUTERIE BOARD

DESKA WĘDLIN Z SOSEM CHRZANOWYM

Polish charcuterie takes on a completely different flavor when grilled. If you live near a Polish deli, you can ask them for their recommendations on which ones to serve warm, or simply look for *kabanosy*—the long, thin Polish sausages—or a ring of *kiełbasa*, a smoked Polish sausage. This is one of my favorite boards to offer when friends come over. Serve with plenty of fresh rye bread, pickles, and a horseradish-spiked sauce or a mild mustard. If you can't find fresh horseradish to make the horseradish sauce yourself, you can use any store-bought creamy horseradish sauce. If you happen to have some vodka in your freezer, that would go very well too.

Serves 4

1 lb 5 oz/600 g *kabanos* (smoked
    pork sausage) or 1 ring
    kiełbasa, scored
1 tbsp vegetable oil
1 loaf of rye bread
butter
a selection of pickled cucumbers

For the horseradish sauce
⅔ cup/150 ml sour cream or
    mayonnaise
1 in/2–3 cm piece of fresh
    horseradish root, peeled and
    finely grated
1 tsp sugar
pinch sea salt

Preheat a large frying pan, skillet, or griddle (or you could grill the sausage over a hot barbecue). Brush the pan with a little vegetable oil and fry the sausages for 8–10 minutes, turning occasionally, until warmed all the way through. If you are using a ring of Polish sausage, slice into chunks with a sharp knife once heated.

To make the sauce, mix the sour cream or mayonnaise with the horseradish, adding the sugar and salt.

Slice the bread and butter generously. Serve the grilled sausage on a large board with the bread, pickles, and horseradish sauce.

Right: A typical Polish gent, dressed up in his best coat, enjoying grilled sausage and bread at the street food market on a cold November day in Warsaw.

FOOD FOR FAMILY AND FRIENDS

PRZEPISY DLA RODZINY I PRZYJACIÓŁ

Many of the recipes in this chapter are the recipes I turn to time and again when cooking for my family. Others are "request recipes" that I call in to my Mama when we are on our way to visit. Weeknight favorites, for us, include Meatballs with mushroom sauce (page 118), Beef goulash with pearl barley (page 135) and Steam-roasted chicken with marjoram (page 140). At weekends, we enjoy the slower process of cooking Braised ribs (page 139) or Cabbage parcels (page 136), a childhood favorite. I have loved being able to preserve these recipes by learning how to cook them for myself, as well as developing the confidence to adapt them by simplifying them or lightening them up whenever possible.

I have also included some recipes that have inspired me during recent trips to Poland: Venison with roasted pumpkin purée and Pierogi with wild mushrooms and cream were two of the dishes I enjoyed in Warsaw and which I hadn't tasted before.

The use of grains such as buckwheat, pearl barley, and millet has become commonplace in my cooking and it's great to see these grains becoming more mainstream. We now regularly eat "*kaszotto*" made with barley, and often I'll serve steamed buckwheat instead of rice. We also incorporate plenty of fresh, seasonal vegetables into our cooking, as is common in Poland.

Left: Upstairs, Der Elefant,
Plac Bankowy, Warsaw.

MEATBALLS WITH MUSHROOM SAUCE

KOTLETY MIELONE Z SOSEM PIECZARKOWYM

One of the first recipes I asked my Mama to write down for me when I was leaving home to go to university was her *kotlety mielone*, or meatballs, a dish she often made for supper, served with mashed potatoes and *Mizeria*, or Cucumber and sour cream salad (page 48), and Grated beet salad (page 54) on the side. I missed her cooking so much when I left home. Traditionally, Polish meatballs are coated in breadcrumbs or flour, but I cook mine without to lighten them up. I love eating leftover meatballs in sandwiches with plenty of mayonnaise and dill pickles.

Serves 4

2 tbsp vegetable oil, plus more for
    frying
1 red onion, finely chopped
14 oz/400 g ground beef
14 oz/400 g ground pork
1 egg, beaten
1 tsp mustard
1 tsp dried parsley
½ cup/125 ml beef stock (you can
    use a bouillon cube), cooled
2 slices of bread, preferably
    sourdough rye, soaked in
    a little water
freshly ground black pepper

For the mushroom sauce
1 tsp butter
1 small onion, finely chopped
2½ cups/9 oz/250 g fresh white
    mushrooms, sliced
juice of ½ lemon
½ vegetable or chicken bouillon
    cube, or ½ tsp vegetable
    bouillon powder
1 cup/250 ml light cream

Heat a splash of vegetable oil in a frying pan, add the red onion, and fry for 5 minutes until soft. Leave to cool.

In a large bowl, mix the ground meat, beaten egg, mustard, and parsley. Tip in the cooled onion and pour in the cold stock. Crumble the soaked bread into small pieces and add to the meat. Season the mixture with pepper and mix everything thoroughly with a fork.

Keep a small bowl of cold water nearby, to wet your hands. Take small amounts of the mixture, roughly a tablespoonful at a time, and shape into small balls, then flatten slightly. Between making each meatball, dip your hands in the cold water, to prevent stickiness. You should have enough mixture for 12 meatballs.

In a large frying pan, preferably nonstick, heat the 2 tablespoons of vegetable oil over medium heat. Fry the meatballs, in two batches, for 4 minutes, turning occasionally, until golden all over. Transfer to a plate and continue browning the rest of the meatballs.

Once they are all browned, put the meatballs back into the pan, add 2 tablespoons cold water, shake the pan around a little, cover with a tight-fitting lid or foil, and simmer over low heat for 10 minutes.

To make the mushroom sauce, heat the butter in a frying pan and cook the onion for 5 minutes until soft. Add the mushrooms and lemon juice, and cook for 5 minutes. Crumble in the stock cube and about ½ cup/125 ml of water and simmer for 2 minutes. Add the cream and stir well.

Serve the meatballs and mushroom sauce over mashed potato, with cucumber and sour cream salad and/or grated beet salad on the side.

MILLET "KASZOTTO" WITH WILD MUSHROOMS

KASZA JAGLANA Z GRZYBAMI

A risotto, of course, is a classic Italian dish made with a very particular type of rice. *"Kaszotto"* is a Polish variation, using millet, or *kasza jaglana*. which can be used in place of rice in a very similar way to making a risotto. The texture is different and the *"kaszotto"* is less creamy, but it is lighter and a really good alternative. You can try this with different types of *kasza*; for example, pearl barley groats (*kasza jęczmienna perłowa*) work really well.

Serves 4

1 cup/7 oz/200 g millet
  (*kasza jaglana*)
1 tbsp vegetable oil
1 white onion, finely chopped
1 celery stick, diced
1 garlic clove, finely chopped
4 cups/1 liter
  vegetable stock
¾ oz/20 g dried mushrooms
14 oz/400 g mixed fresh wild
  mushrooms, cleaned and
  chopped
1 tsp butter
2 tsp chopped fresh parsley
sea salt and freshly ground
  black pepper

Using a sieve, rinse the millet until the water runs clear, then drain.

Heat the oil in a large, wide pan, preferably cast-iron. Add the onion, celery, and garlic, and cook over low heat for 10 minutes, until the vegetables are soft and translucent.

Add the drained millet and stir well so that all the grains are coated in oil.

In a separate pan, bring the stock to a gentle boil. Add the dried mushrooms. Add a ladleful of the hot stock to the pan with the millet, stirring until almost all of the liquid has been absorbed before adding another ladleful—leave the mushrooms in the stock to flavor it. Keep going until all the stock has been absorbed. The millet should soften after 10–15 minutes.

Remove the mushrooms from the stock pan using a slotted spoon. Chop them and add to the millet pan. Stir in the fresh wild mushrooms and cook for 5 minutes.

Stir in the butter and parsley, and season with salt and pepper. The *"kaszotto"* shouldn't be too dry and there should still be a bit of a bite to the grains. Serve hot.

BARLEY GROATS WITH ROASTED ZUCCHINI AND ASPARAGUS

KASZA JĘCZMIENNA PERŁOWA Z CUKINIĄ I SZPARAGAMI

This is another tasty alternative to an Italian risotto, here made with barley groats.
The grains give a slightly different texture to an Italian risotto, but the overall dish is lighter and healthier.
You can try this with buckwheat, too.

Serves 4

1 lb 5 oz/600 g zucchini, cubed
9 oz/250 g asparagus, stalks
    trimmed and reserved, stems
    sliced on the diagonal
1 tbsp vegetable oil,
    plus extra for drizzling
    over the vegetables
grated zest of 1 lemon
1 garlic clove, grated
1 white onion, finely chopped
1 cup/7 oz/200 g barley groats
    (*kasza jęczmienna perłowa*)
4 cups/1 liter vegetable stock
sea salt and freshly ground
    black pepper
1 tsp butter
2 tsp chopped fresh parsley

Preheat the oven to 400°F/200°C. Scatter the zucchini and asparagus (saving the trimmed woody ends) on a large baking tray lined with parchment paper. Drizzle over a little oil and scatter over the lemon zest and garlic. Roast for 15 minutes, then set to one side.

Heat 1 tablespoon of oil in a large, wide pan, preferably cast-iron. Add the onion and cook over low heat for 10 minutes, until soft and translucent. Add the barley and stir well so that the grains are coated in oil.

In a separate pan, bring the stock to a gentle boil. Add the trimmed ends of the asparagus stalks. Add a ladleful of the hot stock to the barley (leaving the asparagus trimmings in to flavor the stock), stirring until almost all of the liquid has been absorbed before adding another ladleful. Keep going until all the stock has been absorbed. The barley will take around 15 minutes to cook and soften.

Taste to check it is cooked and season with salt and pepper. Stir in the roasted zucchini and asparagus. Add the butter and parsley, stir, and serve.

PEARL BARLEY RISOTTO WITH BACON AND ROASTED PUMPKIN

RISOTTO Z KASZY PĘCZAK, Z BOCZKIEM I DYNIĄ

This is a "risotto" made with the traditional pearl barley that you might add to soups and stews. You can experiment with other grains—buckwheat makes a nice alternative. With the addition of bacon and pumpkin, this is a wonderfully comforting autumnal dish.

Serves 4

12 oz/350 g pumpkin or
    butternut squash, peeled,
    seeded, and cubed
1 tbsp olive or canola oil,
    plus extra for drizzling on the
    pumpkin
1 garlic clove, grated
3 sprigs of fresh thyme or marjoram
1 white onion, finely chopped
1 carrot, diced
1 celery stick, diced
3½ oz/100 g Polish bacon, *boczek*,
    or *kabanos* smoked sausage,
    or pancetta
1 cup/7 oz/200 g pearl barley
    (*kaszy pęczak*)
4 cups/1 liter vegetable stock,
    made with vegetable bouillon
    powder
1 tbsp almond milk or heavy cream
    (optional)
sea salt and freshly ground
    black pepper
1 tsp butter

Preheat the oven to 400°F/200°C. Scatter the pumpkin or butternut squash on a large baking tray lined with parchment paper. Drizzle over a little of the oil and scatter over the garlic and sprigs of thyme or marjoram. Roast for 20 minutes then set to one side.

Heat 1 tablespoon of the oil in a large, wide pan, preferably cast-iron. Add the onion, carrot, and celery, and cook for 10 minutes until soft and translucent. Add the bacon, *kabanos*, or pancetta and cook for a further 5 minutes. Add the barley and stir well so that the grains are coated.

In a separate pan, bring the stock to a gentle boil. Add a ladleful of the hot stock to the pan, stirring the barley until almost all of the liquid has been absorbed before adding another ladleful. Keep going until all the stock is absorbed and the barley is tender. The barley may take 40 minutes or more to cook, so use more stock if necessary.

Stir in the roasted pumpkin or butternut squash. Alternatively, you can purée the pumpkin in a blender with a dash of almond milk or cream, and then stir the purée into the barley. Season well with salt and pepper. Add the butter, stir, and serve.

WANDA'S ITALIAN "BIGOS"

BIGOS WŁOSKI WANDZI

My sister, Wanda, lives in Italy and finds it quite hard to source any Polish ingredients. What I love about her cooking is the way that she has learned to adapt the Polish recipes of our childhood to suit her terroir. This is her version of *bigos*, Poland's national dish, but she lightens it up by using pork loin, tenderloin, or ribs, a little pancetta, and plenty of fresh cabbage and tomatoes, making it a lovely dish to eat during the summer months. You could even use turkey fillet. Wanda reminds me of the Italian–Polish Queen Bona Sforza, who married King Sigismund I of Poland in the early 16th century. She missed the cooking of her homeland and decided to bring her Italian cooks to Poland. They planted huge vegetable gardens at Wawel Castle and expanded the use of Italian vegetables within Polish cooking, importing items such as tomatoes and olive oil. My sister doesn't have a royal team of cooks, but she is resourceful nevertheless, and her food is always delicious.

Serves 8

2 tbsp olive oil
2 white onions, finely chopped
3½ oz/100 g pancetta, or Polish
    bacon, *boczek*, or Polish
    sausage, *kabanos*, finely sliced
1 lb/450 g pork loin or tenderloin,
    or meaty pork ribs, or turkey fillet,
    chopped into ½ in/1 cm cubes
3 cups/14 oz/400 g sauerkraut,
    preferably organic, drained
    and rinsed
sea salt and freshly ground
    black pepper
1 bay leaf, preferably fresh
2 cups/475 ml homemade
    or good-quality chicken or
    vegetable stock, plus more if
    needed
14 oz/400 g (5 large) ripe plum
    or other seasonal tomatoes
1 pointed (sweetheart, hispi)
    cabbage or ½ fresh white
    cabbage
1 red apple
1½ cups/5½ oz/150 g mushrooms,
    chopped

Preheat the oven to 350°F/180°C. In a large cast-iron pan or Dutch oven, heat the olive oil over low heat. Add the onions and pancetta, and cook for 10 minutes until the onions soften (don't let them burn).

Turn up the heat under the pan and add the pork or turkey to brown it all over. This will take 5–6 minutes and the pork and onions will start to turn golden brown and sticky.

On a chopping board, chop the sauerkraut (which tends to be a bit long and stringy) and then add it to the pan of onions and pork. Season with salt and pepper, then add the bay leaf. Pour in 1 cup/250 ml of the stock. Cover the pan with a lid or foil and place in the oven for 1 hour.

Meanwhile, put the tomatoes in a large bowl and cover them with freshly boiled water. After about 30 seconds, drain and cover them with cold water. Drain again; it should now be easy to peel off the skins. Cut the tomatoes in half and scoop out the seeds, then chop the flesh into small cubes, and set aside. Core and finely chop the cabbage, removing any tough outer leaves. Peel and grate the apple.

Remove the pan from the oven and add a layer of tomatoes. Top with the mushrooms, apple, and cabbage. Season with salt and pepper and pour in another 1 cup/250 ml of the stock.

Cover the pan and put it back into the oven for 30 minutes.

Stir and check the liquid—it should not be too dry, so you may need to add a little more stock. Put the pan back into the oven for a further 1 hour. The *bigos* will be ready to eat after this time, but will taste better if left to cool completely, and reheated the next day over medium heat.

POLISH GNOCCHI WITH BACON AND MUSHROOMS

KOPYTKA Z BOCZKIEM I GRZYBAMI

Kopytka translates as "little hooves," and they are sometimes described as Polish gnocchi because they are similar to Italian gnocchi. Some Poles also call these *paluszki*, which means "little fingers." I sometimes experiment with gluten-free flour and I like to make these with almond flour. These can be served sweet, too, with melted butter and a sprinkle of sugar, drizzle of honey or maple syrup—even for breakfast. If you add *twaróg*, Polish soft cheese, to the dough, you end up with *leniwe*, "lazy dumplings." In the Ukraine, these are made simply with cheese, egg, and flour and called *halushky*.

Serves 4

1 lb 2 oz/500 g russet potatoes,
    peeled
sea salt and freshly ground
    black pepper
2 cups/9 oz/250 g all-purpose flour,
    plus extra for dusting
    (or use almond flour for a
    gluten-free version)
1 egg, beaten

To serve
vegetable or olive oil
1 tsp butter
1 onion, finely chopped
3½ oz/100 g Polish bacon, *boczek*,
    or pancetta
3½ cups/7 oz/200 g fresh
    chanterelles, or porcini, or
    chestnut mushrooms
2 tsp chopped fresh parsley

Boil the potatoes in a large pan of salted water until very soft. Drain and set aside to steam dry. Once cool and very dry, mash until smooth. Leave the potatoes to cool completely or chill in the fridge.

Put the cold mashed potatoes into a large bowl. Add the flour, beaten egg, and a good pinch of salt and pepper. Using a metal spoon, bring the mixture together, then tip it out onto a lightly floured board or work surface and knead until all the flour is incorporated into the potatoes. The dough should be fairly soft and springy, but not too sticky.

Sprinkle a little more flour onto the board and cut the dough into quarters. Roll each piece into a long cylinder and cut the dough at an angle into 1 in/2–3 cm pieces. Repeat until you have used up all the dough.

Bring a saucepan of salted water to a boil and drop a few dumplings in at a time—it's best to cook them in batches. Gently boil for 3–4 minutes; they will rise to the top once cooked. Take them out with a slotted spoon, drain in a colander, and continue until you have cooked all the dumplings. Set them aside.

Heat the oil and butter in a large frying pan and cook the onions for 4–5 minutes until soft. Add the bacon and fry until golden and crisp. Add the mushrooms, season with salt and pepper, and stir in the parsley. Add the *kopytka* to the pan, stir everything together, and cook until the *kopytka* begin to turn golden, then serve.

POTATO PANCAKES WITH MUSHROOM SAUCE

PLACKI ZIEMNIACZANE Z SOSEM GRZYBOWYM

Polish potato pancakes are like latkes, in that they are made with potatoes, grated onion, and egg, then pan-fried. I make mine with gluten-free flour, but you can use ordinary all-purpose flour. If you are Polish, *placki* will be a throwback to your childhood. Favorite toppings include a little butter and sour cream. They go very well with the mushroom sauce given here or with Beef goulash (page 135) but you can also serve them sweet, with apple sauce and/or cream and sprinkled with sugar. For savory pancakes, add the onion and leave out the apple. If you want to serve *placki* with sweet toppings, such as sour cream and sugar, then add the apple instead of the onion.

My best friend, Monika, got me into eating *placki* with a raw salad, or *surówka*, on the side recently and I think this really livens them up. Try the White cabbage and carrot slaw (page 52) or Grated beet salad (page 54). You can keep the pancakes warm on a plate covered in foil in a low oven for up to 30 minutes.

Serves 4 (about 10 pancakes)

about 1 lb 7 oz/650 g (4 large)
   baking potatoes, peeled
1 small red onion (if serving savory
   pancakes)
1 apple (if serving sweet pancakes)
1 egg, beaten
2 tbsp gluten-free flour blend,
   potato flour, or all-purpose flour
sea salt and freshly ground
   black pepper
3 tbsp vegetable oil, for frying
chopped fresh dill, to garnish

For the mushroom sauce
1 tbsp vegetable oil
1 small onion, finely chopped
2½ cups/9 oz/250 g white
   mushrooms, sliced
juice of ½ lemon
scant ½ cup/100 ml vegetable or
   chicken stock
1 cup/250 ml light cream
   or sour cream

Using the coarse side of a box grater, grate the potatoes and place them in a sieve or colander set over a bowl to allow some of the excess liquid to drain. Grate the onion or apple and add it to the potato. Leave to stand for 10 minutes.

Meanwhile, make the sauce. Heat the oil in a frying pan over low heat and fry the onion for 10 minutes, until golden and soft. Add the mushrooms and cook for a further 2 minutes, until soft. Add the lemon juice. Pour in the stock and simmer for 1 minute, then stir in the cream and leave to bubble and simmer for 2–3 minutes, until slightly thickened.

Using the back of a spoon, or your hands, squeeze out most of the excess liquid from the potato mixture. Put the potato mixture into a large bowl. Add the beaten egg and flour, and season with salt and pepper, then stir everything together—the mixture should be quite thick and not too dry.

Heat a little vegetable oil in a large frying pan over medium heat. Take a small handful of the mixture and flatten it in the palm of your hand to make a pancake about 3½ in/8–9 cm in diameter. Carefully place in the hot oil and repeat: you should be able to fit four or five *placki* in the pan. Cook for 2–3 minutes, until golden, then flip and cook the other side. Transfer the *placki* to a plate lined with paper towels to drain. Repeat until all the potato mixture is used, adding a little more oil if necessary.

Serve the pancakes with the mushroom sauce, garnish with dill, and serve a raw salad on the side.

VEAL CHOPS WITH CHERRY VODKA SAUCE

KOTLETY CIELĘCE Z SOSEM WIŚNIOWYM

Veal has seen something of a comeback, with new ethical farming standards in place, although it has always been popular in Polish cooking. For this recipe you can use bone-in veal chops, veal medallions, or veal tenderloin. Always look for high-welfare, ethically reared meat. This goes particularly well with any of the salads, or *surówki*, in Chapter 2. If you can't find fresh cherries, veal also goes really well with the mushroom sauce (served with the meatballs) on page 118 and perhaps a little steamed buckwheat.

Serves 4

4 veal chops or steaks
2 tbsp olive oil
1 tbsp fresh or dried marjoram
   or thyme
juice of ½ lemon
1 garlic clove, crushed

For the cherry vodka sauce
9 oz/250 g fresh cherries, pitted
2½ tbsp (1 shot) vodka (use cherry
   vodka if you have some)
3 tbsp chicken stock
1 tbsp clear honey
1 garlic clove, crushed
sea salt and freshly ground
   black pepper
½ tsp cornstarch or arrowroot,
   mixed with a little water

Place the veal chops in a flat dish or tray. In a small bowl, mix the olive oil, marjoram or thyme, lemon juice, and garlic and spread over the veal. Cover the dish with plastic wrap and place in the fridge for at least 2 hours, or overnight.

When ready to cook, take the veal chops out of the fridge, leaving them in the marinade for 10 minutes to bring them to room temperature.

Meanwhile, make the sauce. In a small saucepan, combine the cherries, vodka, stock, honey, and garlic, and cook over low heat for 10 minutes. Taste and season with a little salt and pepper. Stir in the cornstarch mixture and bring to a boil, until the sauce thickens slightly. Set to one side.

Heat a large frying pan or a griddle pan. Once hot, add the veal chops and cook for 5 minutes on each side, until golden. Remove the chops from the pan and place them on a plate. Cover with foil and leave to rest for 5 minutes, pouring any resulting juices into the cherry sauce. Stir the sauce and reheat it gently if necessary. Serve the veal chops on a plate with the cherry vodka sauce.

VENISON WITH ROASTED PUMPKIN AND THYME PURÉE

DZICZYZNA Z PIECZONĄ DYNIĄ I TYMIANKIEM

I became a convert to venison when I ate it in a restaurant in Warsaw recently. There is plenty of wild game in Poland, and the chef, Marek, had been hunting; he prepared a beautiful tenderloin steak served with puréed pumpkin, kale, and braised lentils. This is the way I recreate the dish at home; it makes a wonderful autumn or winter dinner-party dish, served with leafy greens, such as kale or rainbow chard. Venison has less fat than a skinless chicken breast, is high in iron, and has plenty of healthy omega-3 fats. Choose free-range or wild venison, not farmed.

Serves 4

3 tbsp vegetable oil,
   preferably organic
1 pumpkin or butternut squash,
   peeled, seeded, and cubed
bunch of fresh thyme, leaves picked
sea salt and freshly ground
   black pepper
⅔ cup/150 ml chicken stock,
   preferably homemade
1 tsp butter
⅔ cup/150 ml heavy cream
4 venison steaks

Preheat the oven to 400°F/200°C. Line a large baking sheet with parchment paper, drizzle over 1 tablespoon of the oil, and scatter on the pumpkin and thyme leaves. Season with salt and pepper and drizzle over some more oil. Roast for 20 minutes or until the pumpkin is golden brown on the outside and soft in the middle. Transfer the cooked pumpkin to a food processor, process to a purée, and loosen with the stock, adding the butter and the cream.

Heat a large frying pan over high heat. Rub the venison steaks with the remaining oil and season both sides with salt and pepper. Sear the steaks in the hot pan for 3–4 minutes on each side, until cooked to your liking. Remove from the pan and leave the steaks to rest for a few minutes, then serve with the pumpkin purée and some wilted greens.

GLUTEN-FREE BREADED PORK STEAKS

KOTLET SCHABOWY BEZGLUTENOWY

Breaded pork steaks, sometimes called *kotlet schabowy* or *kotlet babci*, are one of my favorite childhood dishes. To lighten them up, I use almond flour and gluten-free breadcrumbs, and lean pork steaks. These go very well with Wanda's Italian "bigos" (page 125) or with any of the raw salads in Chapter 2, and they make a great low-carb weeknight dinner. You can also make these with chicken breast in place of the pork.

Serves 4

4 lean boneless pork steaks,
   preferably organic
sea salt and freshly ground
   black pepper
⅔ cup/4½ oz/125 g almond flour
   or gluten-free flour blend
1 egg, beaten
2 cups/5½ oz/150 g dried
   breadcrumbs, or 1 cup/2 oz/60 g
   fresh gluten-free breadcrumbs
light vegetable oil,
   for shallow-frying

Bring the pork steaks to room temperature. Wrap them loosely in plastic wrap, then bash them with a rolling pin to flatten. Season the steaks on both sides with salt and pepper.

Put the flour, beaten egg, and breadcrumbs onto three separate plates. Heat ½ in/1 cm of oil in a large frying pan.

Taking one steak at a time, dip it into the flour until well coated, then into the egg, and then into the breadcrumbs. Press the meat into the breadcrumbs to make sure the steaks are covered all over.

Place the breaded steaks into the hot oil and fry for 6 minutes on each side, until golden brown and cooked all the way through. Serve with *bigos* or a raw salad on the side.

BEEF GOULASH WITH PEARL BARLEY

GULASZ WOŁOWY Z KASZĄ JĘCZMIENNĄ

Goulash is, of course, well known as one of the national dishes of Hungary, but the Poles have their own version, usually made with beef. This is a great dish to cook in your slow cooker, or you can cook it in a cast-iron pan over low heat. I recently had this in a traditional Polish restaurant in Warsaw, with a sweet local wine, similar to a Riesling. The goulash was served with pearl barley, which I thought made a nice alternative to rice or potatoes. This recipe has also become a firm favorite at our school's Christmas Fair, served with homemade Irish soda bread.

Serves 4

2 tbsp vegetable oil,
    preferably organic
2 large onions, chopped
1 lb 2 oz/500 g beef chuck or other
    stewing cuts, cubed
2 red peppers, seeded
    and chopped
2 ripe tomatoes, peeled, seeded,
    and chopped
2 tbsp tomato paste
2 tsp paprika
2 tbsp all-purpose flour
2 cups/500 ml hot beef
    stock
sea salt and freshly ground
    black pepper
2 bay leaves, preferably fresh
1 cup/7 oz/200 g pearl barley
    groats (*kasza jęczmienna
    perłowa*)
2 tbsp chopped fresh parsley
about ⅔ cup/150 ml sour cream,
    to serve

Heat the oil in a large cast-iron pan or Dutch oven, add the onions, and cook over low heat for 10 minutes, until soft and translucent.

Turn up the heat, add the beef, and cook for 5 minutes to brown all over. Add the red peppers, stir, and cook for 2 minutes, then reduce the heat to low. Add the tomatoes, tomato paste, and paprika, and stir.

In a cup, mix the flour with 2 tablespoons cold water and then add this to the pan. Pour in the hot beef stock, stir, and season well with salt and pepper. Add the bay leaves.

Cover the pan with a lid and simmer for 1½–2 hours over low heat, stirring occasionally. Or transfer to a slow cooker and cook on medium–low for 4–5 hours.

Cook the pearl barley according to the package instructions. Serve the goulash with the barley, sprinkle with parsley, and serve with the sour cream on the side.

CABBAGE PARCELS WITH BARLEY AND MUSHROOM SAUCE

GOŁĄBKI Z KASZĄ PERŁOWĄ, W SOSIE PIECZARKOWYM

Stuffed cabbage parcels or rolls, called *gołąbki*, "little pigeons," are very popular in Poland. They can be made with rice and ground meat and served with tomato sauce (see instructions overleaf), or, as in this recipe, with barley and mushroom sauce. They make a lovely main course for vegetarian visitors and you can prepare them in advance. I like to use crushed barley groats (*kasza jęczmienna perłowa*), but you could also make these with buckwheat, which would make them gluten free. In Poland, and at my local Polish shop during the spring, you can buy really large white cabbages, but to make 12 parcels you may need the outer leaves of two white cabbages.

Serves 4

¾ cup/5½ oz/150 g pearl barley groats, buckwheat, or white rice
sea salt and freshly ground black pepper
4 lb/2 kg white cabbage, (2 medium-large)
1 oz/30 g dried mushrooms
2 tbsp vegetable oil
1 white onion, finely chopped
14 oz/400 g fresh mixed wild or cultivated mushrooms, chopped
2 tsp dried marjoram
2 cups/500 ml vegetable stock

For the mushroom sauce
1 tsp butter
1 small onion, finely chopped
2½ cups/9 oz/250 g white mushrooms, sliced
juice of ½ lemon
1 cup/250 ml vegetable stock
1 cup/250 ml light cream

Cook the barley, buckwheat, or rice according to the package instructions, but take 4 minutes off the cooking time so that the grains are al dente. Drain and leave to cool completely.

Bring a large pan of water to a boil and then turn the heat down so that the water is just simmering. Add a large pinch of salt. Remove the outer leaves of the cabbage and keep these to one side.

Put the whole cabbage into the pan and simmer for 10 minutes to blanch. This will help the leaves to come away more easily. Carefully remove the cabbage from the boiling water, leave it to cool down a little, and then, using a sharp knife, score around the core and pull away the outer leaves, one by one, making sure the leaves stay whole.

When the leaves start to get trickier to remove, put the cabbage back into the hot water for a few minutes, then take it out and repeat the process of scoring the core and gently pulling away the leaves.

Put the dried mushrooms into a cup or small bowl, pour over some boiling water, and leave to soak.

Heat the oil in a large frying pan, add the onions, and cook over low heat for 10 minutes until soft. Add the fresh mushrooms and cook for a further 5 minutes. Drain the rehydrated mushrooms (reserving the liquid), chop them, and add to the pan.

Continued_

Add the marjoram and season well with salt and pepper.

Add the mushroom mixture to the cooked grains, adding 2 tablespoons of the reserved mushroom soaking liquid—this is your filling.

Preheat the oven to 400°F/200°C. Line a baking tray with the reserved outer leaves of the cabbage.

Taking one blanched cabbage leaf at a time, cut out the thick part of the core. Put a heaped tablespoon of the filling onto the cabbage leaf, fold in the sides, and then roll up the cabbage leaf to form a parcel.

Place each cabbage roll, seam-side down, into the baking tray, packing them as tightly as you can. Pour the stock into the tray around the cabbage parcels. Cover the tray with foil and bake for 1 hour.

After an hour, remove the foil and bake uncovered for 10 minutes.

While the cabbage parcels are in the oven, make the mushroom sauce. Heat the butter in a frying pan and fry the onion for 5 minutes, until soft. Add the mushrooms and lemon juice, and cook for a further 5 minutes. Pour in the stock and simmer for 2 minutes. Add the cream and simmer for 5 minutes. Serve the cabbage rolls with the sauce.

GOŁĄBKI Z MIĘSEM

CABBAGE PARCELS WITH RICE AND MEAT
Cook ¾ cup/5½ oz/150 g white rice according to the package instructions, but take 4 minutes off the cooking time so that the grains are al dente. Drain and leave to cool completely. Put 14 oz/400 g ground pork, or a mixture of ground pork and veal, into a large bowl. Season very well with salt and pepper. Tip in the rice. Add an egg and mix everything together well; use this as your filling. Follow the process above for removing and filling the cabbage leaves. Although these are traditionally served with a fresh tomato sauce, they go well with the mushroom sauce, too.

RIBS WITH HONEY AND VODKA

ŻEBERKA Z MIODEM I WÓDKĄ

This is one of my favorite Friday-night suppers. There are so many wonderful raw, organic honeys available now that it's worth experimenting: I've made these with raw thyme-infused honey and with wildflower honey. Use a good-quality vodka, too, and the best meaty ribs you can find—pork or beef. Short ribs and racks work well, too. This is my brother Roman's method of cooking ribs—and they always turn out so wonderfully tender.

Serves 4

2¼ lb/1 kg baby back ribs or
    individual pork or beef ribs
6 cups/1.5 liters chicken or beef
    stock

For the honey vodka sauce
½ cup/125 ml clear honey
scant ½ cup/100 ml
    good-quality vodka
¼ cup/60 ml soy sauce
2 tbsp red wine vinegar
2 tsp Dijon mustard
2 tsp tomato ketchup

Preheat the oven to 350°F/180°C.

Place the ribs in a large saucepan, big enough to hold the rack or all of the ribs. Pour the stock over the ribs. Place the pan over low heat and very gently simmer (don't boil) the ribs for 30 minutes.

While the ribs are simmering, make the honey vodka sauce by putting the ingredients into a bowl or jug and whisking together well.

After 30 minutes, carefully lift the ribs out of the stock and put them into a baking tray or roasting pan. Pour the honey vodka sauce over the ribs. Measure out 1 cup/250 ml of the stock from the pan and pour into the pan with the ribs. (You can strain the remaining stock and use it to make soup.) Cover the pan with foil and place in the oven for 30 minutes.

Take the ribs out of the oven and remove the foil. Carefully spoon the sauce over the ribs. Put the ribs back in the oven, uncovered, for a further 15 minutes, until they begin to brown.

Take the ribs out of the oven. Cover again with foil and leave to stand for at least 15 minutes before serving. If you have used a rack of ribs, separate the ribs to serve.

STEAM-ROASTED CHICKEN WITH MARJORAM

KURCZAK PIECZONY Z MAJERANKIEM

The secret to a perfectly cooked, "falling-apart" roast chicken, as I have learned from my sister Elizabeth, is to add vegetables and water to the roasting pan, cover it, and cook it at a slightly lower-than-normal heat, but for a longer cooking time—essentially leaving your chicken in the oven for 2–3 hours. The vegetables and chicken juices make for a delicious gravy. Marjoram, fresh or dried, adds a wonderful sweet herby Polish flavor. I serve my roast chicken with cracked pearl barley or buckwheat *kasza* and at least two raw salads (see Chapter 2).

Serves 4

1 large chicken, preferably
    free-range, organic
4 carrots, halved lengthways
2 white onions, halved, outer
    skin removed
2 tbsp vegetable oil
sea salt and freshly ground
    black pepper
1 tsp chicken seasoning,
    a crumbled bouillon cube, or
    1 tsp bouillon powder
2 tbsp fresh or dried marjoram
1 cup/250 ml water

To make gravy (optional)
1 tbsp all-purpose flour
1 cup/250 ml chicken stock

Take the chicken out of the fridge about 20 minutes before you start cooking.

Preheat the oven to 400°F/200°C.

Put the carrots and onions into a large cast-iron pan or deep roasting pan and place the chicken on top. Drizzle with the oil and season well with salt, pepper, the chicken seasoning or bouillon powder, and marjoram. Pour the water around the chicken and cover the pan with a lid or tightly with foil.

Place the chicken in the oven for 20 minutes. Reduce the oven temperature to 350°F/180°C and continue to cook for a further 2 hours. After this time, remove the lid or foil, turn the oven back up to 400°F/200°C, and cook for a further 20 minutes, or until the skin is golden and crisp.

Once cooked (test by piercing with a thin skewer—the juices should run clear, not pink), take the chicken out of the oven, cover it with foil, and leave to rest for 15 minutes.

Remove the carrots and onions from the pan and save them, along with the chicken carcass, to make a stock later. Or use them, along with the juices in the pan, to make some gravy, first removing any fat with a tablespoon, or using a gravy separator jug. Mash the vegetables with a fork or a potato masher. Add the flour and stir until thickened. Pour in chicken stock, strain, then bring to a boil again before serving.

Carve the chicken and serve with cracked pearl barley or buckwheat *kasza* and fresh vegetables, or a couple of raw salads.

DUCK BREASTS WITH PLUM, HONEY, AND RED WINE SAUCE

PIERŚ KACZKI Z SOSEM ŚLIWKOWYM, MIODEM I CZERWONYM WINEM

In Poland, the kind of plums that you use to make sauces or jams are called *śliwki węgierki*, which are deep purple damsons, but you can use any ripe purple plums. You can also make this sauce with cherries, and it goes equally well with duck or roast chicken. Serve with White cabbage and carrot slaw (page 52), or any of the raw salads (*surówki*) in Chapter 2.

Serves 4

4 duck breasts with skin
sea salt and freshly ground
   black pepper

For the sauce
1 tsp vegetable oil,
   preferably organic
1 tsp butter
1 shallot, finely chopped
7 oz/200 g plums (3 medium),
   pitted and chopped
1 cup/250 ml red wine
⅔ cup/150 ml chicken stock,
   preferably homemade
2 tbsp honey
1 tsp *powidła* (Polish plum butter,
   page 44) (optional)
½ tsp cornstarch, mixed with a little
   water

Preheat the oven to 425°F/220°C.

Score the duck breasts and season them with salt and pepper. Put the duck in a cold dry frying pan, skin-side down, and place the pan over medium heat for 6 minutes, keeping the breasts skin-side down.

Transfer the duck to a baking tray and place in the oven for 10 minutes (rare) or 15 minutes (medium). Remove the duck breasts from the oven, put them on a plate, and leave to rest in a warm place for 10 minutes.

To make the sauce, heat the oil and butter in a saucepan over low heat, add the shallot, and cook for 5 minutes until soft. Add the plums and cook for a further 2 minutes. Add the wine, stock, and honey, and *powidła* if using. Stir well, add the cornstarch mixture, and cook for 10 minutes. Take off the heat and either pass the sauce through a sieve or pureé in a food processor.

Slice the duck breasts and serve with the plum sauce.

ROAST DUCK LEGS WITH APPLES AND POTATOES

PIECZONE UDKA KACZKI Z JABŁKAMI I ZIEMNIAKAMI

Roast duck with apples is a classic Polish dish, usually made during the hunting season. At home, I tend to make this with four duck legs, and I often double the recipe so I have leftover duck meat to shred, and apples, for filling pierogi (page 150). You can also make this using a whole duck, or goose. This recipe is a fabulous one-pan meal to feed a crowd.

Serves 4

4 duck legs
6 eating apples
1 white onion, quartered
1 lb 2 oz/500 g potatoes, peeled and chopped into large cubes
sea salt and freshly ground black pepper
2 tsp caraway seeds
2 tsp dried marjoram
1 cup/250 ml freshly boiled water

Preheat the oven to 350°F/180°C.

Score the duck legs (or pierce the skin) with a sharp knife. Place them in a large frying pan (without any oil) over low heat and gently increase the heat so that the duck legs start to become brown all over and some of the fat begins to render. This will take around 10 minutes.

Meanwhile, peel and core the apples and arrange them in a large baking tray, along with the onion and potatoes.

Transfer the duck from the pan to the baking tray. Season well with salt and pepper, and sprinkle with the caraway seeds and marjoram. Pour the freshly boiled water over the duck. Cover the tray with foil and place in the oven to roast for 1 hour.

Remove the foil, give everything a good stir, and roast for a further 30 minutes. Take the tray out of the oven carefully and leave the duck to rest for 10 minutes before serving.

ROASTED PORK CHOPS
WITH BABY CARROTS AND CARAWAY

KOTLET SCHABOWY PIECZONY Z MARCHEWKĄ I KMINKIEM

Pork, carrots, and caraway have a wonderful affinity and this is such an easy weeknight supper.
During the spring months, I like to add a few spears of asparagus. Finish the dish with plenty of fresh dill.

Serves 4

4 thick-cut pork chops
10½ oz/300 g baby carrots,
    washed and topped
1 lb 2 oz/500 g small potatoes
2 tbsp vegetable oil,
    preferably organic
2 tsp caraway seeds
about 1 lb/450 g asparagus
    (if in season)
2 tbsp clear honey
sea salt and freshly ground
    black pepper
chopped fresh dill, to serve

Preheat the oven to 400°F/200°C. Take the pork chops out of the
fridge at least 20 minutes before cooking.

Put the carrots and potatoes into a large roasting pan, drizzle with
1 tablespoon of the oil, and sprinkle over the caraway seeds. Roast in
the oven for 20 minutes.

Heat the remaining 1 tablespoon of oil in a large frying pan. Fry the
pork chops for 4 minutes each side until they start to turn golden
brown. Add them to the roasting pan, along with the asparagus and
honey, and season with salt and pepper.

Place in the oven for a further 20 minutes and roast until the pork is
cooked through. Remove the tray from the oven and leave everything
to rest for 10 minutes. Scatter with chopped dill and serve.

PAN-ROASTED COD WITH LEEKS AND CREAM

DORSZ Z POREM I ŚMIETANĄ

The delicate flavor of cod goes beautifully with leeks. I always serve this with new potatoes, topped with butter and plenty of fresh dill (see page 89), as well as a couple of the raw salads in Chapter 2.

Serves 4

2 tbsp vegetable oil,
  preferably organic
1 tsp butter
4 cod fillets or loins
2 leeks, outer skin removed,
  white parts finely chopped
generous ¾ cup/200 ml heavy
  cream, or use sour cream for
  a sharper flavor

Heat the oil and butter in a large frying pan and fry the fish for 3 minutes on each side. Add the leeks to the pan and cook for a further 4 minutes. Stir in the cream and spoon some of the cream over the fillets. Cover with a lid and let the sauce bubble for 2 minutes. Serve the fish and creamy leeks with dill buttered new potatoes.

BAKED BREAM WITH DILL BUTTER SAUCE

LESZCZ PIECZONY Z SOSEM KOPERKOWYM

Freshwater bream is fished in the Baltic Sea, along with zander, perch, and cod. I like to bake it very simply and serve it with a dill butter sauce. Most Polish sauce recipes include flour, which gives a slightly thicker sauce, but I prefer mine without. This bream goes particularly well with Asparagus à la Polonaise (page 90), with or without the poached egg.

Serves 4
vegetable oil, preferably organic
4 sea bream fillets or
   2 whole bream
sea salt and freshly ground
   black pepper

For the sauce
2 tbsp butter
a squeeze of lemon juice
2 tbsp chopped fresh dill

Preheat the oven to 350°F/180°C. Line a baking tray with parchment paper.

Drizzle a little oil over the lined baking tray. Season the fish fillets, place them skin-side down on the tray, and bake for 15 minutes. If using whole bream, score the skin diagonally four or five times with a sharp knife, brush with oil, sprinkle with salt, and bake for 20–25 minutes.

To make the sauce, melt the butter in a small saucepan. Squeeze in the lemon juice, season well with salt and pepper, and stir in the fresh dill.

Remove the fish from the oven and spoon over the dill butter sauce to serve.

POLISH DUMPLINGS

PIEROGI

Being Polish and having an insatiable love of pierogi go hand in hand. For me they conjure up images of a big family table, my Mama cooking endless batches, and dishing up these little pockets of dough, filled with potato and cheese or mushrooms, coated in warm butter and caramelized onions and, sometimes, *słonina*, a type of pure pork fat. Pierogi are similar to ravioli and can be savory or sweet—the sweeter versions (page 158) tend to be made during the summer months with seasonal fruits, such as strawberries, blueberries, or sweet plums, sprinkled with sugar, and served with whipped cream. In Polish, the pierogi filling is called the *farsz*. Each year, there is a pierogi pilgrimage in Krakow, a huge street food festival where Poles showcase all sorts of flavors and toppings—from the very traditional to the very modern. I've eaten pierogi recently from a cart in New York City and at a street food festival in London.

The origins of pierogi are hard to trace—they are almost certainly Slavic and there are many variations of them within Polish, Ukrainian, Russian, Lithuanian, and Romanian cuisines. In Lithuania they are known as *vareniki*. In the Ukraine, they are called *varenyky*: yeast is used for the dough and they are steamed. In Russia, *pelmeni* are a slightly smaller dumpling. Note that Russian *piroshky* are usually baked pies rather than boiled dumplings.

There are also comparisons to be drawn with Italian ravioli, given that pierogi are made with a simple dough of flour and water and are filled with a variety of fillings, sweet or savory. They are also almost certainly related to Asian dumplings—Chinese, Mongolian, or even Persian. Sometimes, you might find a dough recipe that includes melted butter, or sour cream. My Mama adds an egg yolk, for extra richness.

Pierogi Ruskie (originating in the Kresy region of Poland, where my father was born) are made with potato and soft white cheese and are probably the most popular filling you'll find (see page 155).

Pierogi with wild mushrooms and sauerkraut are often served on *Wigilia* or Christmas Eve. There are also all kinds of braised meat fillings. I love meat-filled pierogi and have also been known to fill mine with leftover duck and apples from the recipe on page 144. On a recent trip to Poland I visited a *pierogarnia*—a dedicated pierogi restaurant—near the old town in Warsaw, where I had them with a creamy wild mushroom filling—simply delicious.

Continued_

This is my Mama's master recipe, which makes enough dough for approximately 40 pierogi. They are easier to make in one big batch. If you wish to freeze them, it is best to blanch them very quickly in boiling water, drain, and place them flat on a tray so that they don't stick together. Freeze. Once frozen, they can be placed in a freezer bag. To cook, simply add the frozen pierogi to a big pan of boiling water as below.

Makes about 40 pierogi

8 cups/2¼ lb/1 kg all-purpose flour or "00" pasta flour, plus extra for dusting
1 egg, lightly beaten
1 tbsp vegetable oil
1 cup/250 ml lukewarm water

Sift the flour onto a large wooden board or work surface. Make a well in the center and add the beaten egg and the oil, along with a few tablespoons of warm water. Using a knife, begin to mix together, adding a little more water 1 tablespoonful at a time. At first the dough will be quite soft and sticky. Use your hands to bring the dough together into a ball.

Once the dough has come together, knead it on a floured surface for 4–5 minutes. The dough should become quite elastic. If it is too wet, add a little more flour. Put the dough into a bowl, cover with a damp dish towel, and set aside for 30 minutes.

Divide the dough in half and keep one half covered with a damp dish towel to prevent it from drying out. Sprinkle your work surface with flour and roll out the dough until it is about ⅛ in/3 mm thick.

Have a floured tray or board on hand. Using a pastry cutter or an inverted glass tumbler, cut out 3 in/8 cm circles of dough. Continue until all the dough is used. Cover the circles with a damp dish towel until you are ready to start filling—or cut out a few circles at a time and fill them as you go along, keeping the dough covered with a damp dish towel.

To fill: Place a circle of dough in the palm of your hand and add a teaspoon of filling in the center of the circle. Fold the dough over to enclose the filling. Using your thumb and finger, pinch the dough along the edge so that the pierogi is well sealed. Lay the pierogi in rows on the floured tray and cover with a damp dish towel while you make the rest.

To cook the pierogi: Bring a large pan of water to a boil. Carefully drop the dumplings in one at a time (you can probably cook around eight in a standard pan). Keep the water at a gentle boil. The pierogi are cooked when they float up to the top, usually after 2–3 minutes. Lift them out using a slotted spoon, drain in a colander, and set aside while you cook the rest. You can serve the pierogi boiled, as they are, or you can gently fry the boiled pierogi in a frying pan with a little vegetable oil or butter so that they pick up a little golden color.

PIEROGI WITH MUSHROOMS AND CREAM
PIEROGI Z GRZYBAMI I ŚMIETANĄ

1 tsp butter
1 tbsp vegetable oil
1 small onion, finely chopped
1 lb 2 oz/500 g crimini mushrooms,
   finely chopped
2 tsp lemon juice
sea salt and freshly ground black pepper
⅔ cup/150 ml heavy cream
2 tsp chopped fresh parsley

Heat the butter and oil in a frying pan and fry the onion over low heat for 10 minutes, until soft. Add the mushrooms and fry for 5 minutes. Add the lemon juice and season with salt and pepper. Cook until the mushrooms are soft and the pan is almost dry. Stir in the cream and add the parsley. Leave to cool completely before using to fill the pierogi.

PIEROGI WITH BUCKWHEAT, BACON, AND CURD CHEESE
PIEROGI WIEJSKIE Z KASZĄ GRYCZANĄ, BOCZKIEM I TWAROGIEM

⅔ cup/3½ oz/100 g buckwheat, uncooked
2 tbsp vegetable oil
1 white onion, finely chopped
3½ oz/100 g Polish bacon, boczek, or pancetta,
   chopped
7 oz/200 g twaróg, farmer's cheese, or cream cheese
sea salt and freshly ground black pepper
sour cream and chopped fresh chives, to serve

Cook the buckwheat according to the package instructions—usually, this means rinsing the buckwheat and placing it in a pan of cold water, bringing it to a boil, and simmering it for 8 minutes. Drain, rinse, and drain again and leave to cool.

Heat the oil in a large frying pan and cook the onion over low heat for 10 minutes until soft. Add the bacon or pancetta and cook for a further 10 minutes, until crisp.

Tip the onion and bacon into a large bowl with the buckwheat. Stir in the farmer's cheese or cream cheese and leave to cool completely.

Use the mixture to fill the pierogi. Boil and lightly fry the pierogi and serve with a sprinkling of chives and sour cream on the side.

PIEROGI WITH DUCK AND APPLES
PIEROGI Z PIECZONĄ KACZKĄ I JABŁKAMI

Follow the recipe for Roast duck legs with apples and potatoes (page 144)—but leave out the potatoes for this recipe. Once cool enough to handle, shred the duck meat away from the bones. For a slightly finer texture, I like to put the meat into a food processor and pulse it briefly. Alternatively, you can chop the meat very finely with a knife. Mash or purée the cooked apples, add half to the shredded duck meat, and season well with salt and pepper. Leave the filling to cool completely before using to fill the pierogi. Serve the remaining apple purée on the side.

PIEROGI WITH SAUERKRAUT AND WILD MUSHROOMS
PIEROGI Z KISZONĄ KAPUSTĄ I Z GRZYBAMI

1 oz/30 g dried porcini or other dried wild mushrooms
1 tbsp vegetable oil, preferably cold-pressed
1 tsp butter
1 white onion, finely chopped
2½ cups/12 oz/350 g sauerkraut, preferably organic, rinsed, drained, and finely chopped
2 cups/5½ oz/150 g finely chopped wild or crimini mushrooms
½ cup/125 ml vegetable stock
sea salt and freshly ground black pepper

Preheat the oven to 350°F/180°C.

Put the dried porcini into a cup or small bowl, pour over some freshly boiled water, and leave to soak.

Heat the oil and butter in a large frying pan and fry the onion over low heat for 10–15 minutes, until soft and golden. Add the sauerkraut to the onions and cook for 5 minutes. Add the chopped fresh mushrooms. Drain the soaked mushrooms, chop finely, and add them to the sauerkraut. Pour in the stock and season with salt and pepper. Transfer the mixture to a baking dish, cover with foil, and bake for 1 hour.

Remove from the oven and pour out any liquid from the sauerkraut mixture—the filling needs to be dry. Leave to cool, then leave in the fridge overnight before using to fill the pierogi.

PIEROGI WITH CHEESE AND POTATOES
PIEROGI RUSKIE

2¼ lb/1 kg large potatoes, peeled and quartered
sea salt and freshly ground black pepper
10½ oz/300 g *twaróg*, farmer's cheese, or cream cheese
2 tbsp vegetable oil, preferably organic
1 tbsp butter
1 large white onion, very finely chopped

Put the potatoes into a large pan of cold water, add a pinch of salt, and bring the water to a boil over high heat. Turn the heat down and simmer gently for 15 minutes or until the potatoes are soft when pierced with a knife. Drain and leave to dry out completely.

Mash the potatoes, add the farmer's cheese or cream cheese, and mash together—I like to put the mixture through a potato ricer, to make sure the potatoes and cheese are very well combined.

While the potatoes are cooking, heat the oil and butter in a large frying pan. Cook the onion over low heat for at least 10 minutes or until completely soft and slightly caramelized. Leave to cool slightly.

Add the onion to the mashed potato mixture and season well with salt and pepper. Leave to cool completely before filling the pierogi. You can make this filling up to 2 days in advance.

HIGH TEA: SWEET TREATS AND CAKES

PODWIECZOREK NA SŁODKO

It's hard to sum up sweet Polish food in just one chapter, because there is so much to offer! Cakes, tortes, pastries, tarts, yeasted bakes, doughnuts, and cookies—and if you're not tempted by that selection, you can explore sweet desserts such as fruit-filled *pierogi*, cheesecakes, and pancakes. Café culture is strong in Poland. The Poles even have a special time of the day dedicated to eating a sweet treat, called *podwieczorek*, taken around 4pm, between lunch and dinner. This is the perfect time to grab a coffee or lemon tea and sit down with a slice of poppyseed roll, or apple pie.

The flavors common in Polish baking include honey, cinnamon, ginger, and vanilla, as well as dried fruits, such as raisins or citrus peel, while fillings for doughnuts might include plum jam, *powidła*, or rose petal jam. Texture is often added through the use of poppyseeds or nuts. Often a Polish torte will be decorated around the edges with finely chopped nuts. Without doubt there are influences from Eastern Europe, the Turkish spice routes, and French cuisine, particularly in patisserie, though the first pastry shops in Warsaw were opened by Italian and Swiss immigrants. In modern Poland, the American influence is seen in brownies, muffins, and cupcakes.

What I love most about sweet Polish recipes is the way in which fresh fruit so often takes center stage—perhaps the best-loved of Polish cakes is the *szarlotka*, a cake filled with apples, with a crumbly topping. When baking at home, we often begin by going out into the garden to see what we can find: apples, pears, plums, cherries, and fresh currants all feature in my baking, a habit instilled in me from an early age.

When my grandparents first settled in England in the late 1940s, my grandmother would barter for sugar and yeast when the ration van came so she could recreate some of her favorite Polish cakes for her family. I'm pretty sure it is her sweet tooth I have inherited!

PIEROGI WITH STRAWBERRIES, HONEY, AND PISTACHIOS

PIEROGI Z TRUSKAWKAMI, MIODEM I ORZECHAMI PISTACJOWYMI

In Krakow, the old capital city of Poland, there is an annual *pierogi* "street food" festival, now in its sixteenth year. Each year, more and more interesting flavor combinations are showcased, and even though I had tasted sweet pierogi many times before, these strawberry pierogi, lightly fried and drizzled with honey, were particularly memorable. If you are new to making Polish dumplings, or pierogi, then strawberry dumplings are perhaps the simplest to start with, since the strawberries are easy to encapsulate inside the circles of dough. At home, we often made blueberry-filled pierogi, topped with whipped cinnamon cream. Pitted cherries make another wonderful seasonal filling.

Makes about 20 pierogi

2¾ cups/12 oz/350 g all-purpose flour or "00" pasta flour, plus extra for dusting
1 whole egg, plus 1 egg yolk
1 tbsp confectioners' sugar
½ cup/125 ml lukewarm water
1 tbsp vegetable oil

For the filling and topping
2½ cups/12 oz/350 g fresh strawberries, hulled, quartered if large, or halved, if small, or blueberries
2 tbsp unsalted butter
scant ½ cup/100 ml clear honey
¾ cup/1¾ oz/50 g pistachios, finely chopped

In a large bowl, mix the flour, whole egg and yolk, confectioners' sugar, warm water, and oil together.

Tip the dough out onto a lightly floured work surface and knead for about 5 minutes until the dough is no longer sticky and feels smooth. Put the dough back into the bowl, cover with a damp dish towel or plastic wrap, and leave to rest for 30 minutes.

To fill: Divide the dough in half and keep one half covered with a damp dish towel to prevent it from drying out. Sprinkle your work surface with flour, then roll out the dough until it is about ⅛ in/3 mm thick.

Have a floured tray or board on hand. Using a pastry cutter or an inverted glass, cut out 3 in/8 cm circles of dough. Depending on the size of the strawberries, place a couple or a few pieces in the center of each circle. (If using blueberries, 2–3 blueberries will fit.) Fold the dough over to enclose the fruit. Using your thumb and finger, pinch the dough along the edge so that the pierogi is well sealed. Place each dumpling on the floured tray and cover with a damp dish towel while you make the rest.

To cook the pierogi: Bring a large pan of water to a boil. Carefully drop the dumplings in, a few at a time. They will sink at first, but will float up to the top when cooked—this will only take a minute or so.

Continued_

Lift them out using a slotted spoon and place on a plate to cool. If you have sealed them well, none of the filling should have escaped!

Heat the butter in a large frying pan and gently fry the pierogi on both sides until slightly golden. To serve, drizzle with honey and sprinkle with chopped pistachio nuts.

CINNAMON WHIPPED CREAM

Serve this with blueberry-filled pierogi.

1 cup/250 ml heavy cream
1 tbsp confectioners' sugar
1 tsp ground cinnamon
sugar or vanilla sugar, to sprinkle

Whisk the cream with the confectioners' sugar and cinnamon until thickened.

Serve the warm pierogi with a sprinkling of sugar or vanilla sugar and a spoonful (or two) of the cinnamon whipped cream.

POLISH APPLE CAKE

SZARLOTKA

There are lots of different ways to make this traditional Polish cake: every grandmother and aunt will have her own special recipe. The *szarlotka* is really a cross between a cake and a pie, with plenty of apples layered in the middle. I love making this when we have a glut of apples, courtesy of a mature tree we inherited in our garden. This was originally my Mama's recipe, however over the years I have refined my version, reducing the sugar.

You can easily make this a gluten-free cake by using a gluten-free flour blend—the cake is quite crumbly in texture in any case.

Serves 10–12

3½ cups/1 lb/450 g all-purpose
   flour, plus extra for dusting
1 tsp baking powder
scant 1 cup/7 oz/200 g unsalted
   butter, at room temperature,
   plus extra for greasing
grated zest of ½ lemon
generous 1 cup/8 oz/225 g
   superfine sugar
3 egg yolks, plus 1 whole egg,
   at room temperature
1 tbsp plain yogurt
1 tsp vanilla extract or vanilla
   bean paste

For the filling
6 large cooking apples
juice of ½ lemon
¼ cup/1¾ oz/50 g soft brown
   sugar or agave nectar
generous ¾ cup/200 ml water
1 tsp ground cinnamon

To serve
confectioners' sugar,
   for dusting
1 cup/250 ml fresh heavy cream,
   whipped (optional)

Preheat the oven to 350°F/180°C. Grease and line a 9 x 12 in/23 x 30 cm cake pan with parchment paper.

To make the filling, peel, core, and finely slice the apples, tossing the slices with a little lemon juice as you work. Put the apples into a large pan, add the brown sugar or agave nectar, water, and cinnamon. Cook for 5 minutes over a medium heat until just tender, then leave to cool.

To make the dough, put the flour, baking powder, and butter in a food processor and pulse until the mixture is sandy in texture. Add the lemon zest, sugar, egg yolks, whole egg, yogurt, and vanilla. Pulse until the mixture forms a dough. Tip the dough out onto a floured surface, bring it together with your hands, and roll it into a ball.

Divide the dough in half. Wrap one half in plastic wrap and place it in the freezer for 20 minutes.

On a floured surface, roll out the remaining dough and use it to line the baking tray. Press the dough, if necessary, to ensure that it reaches the corners of the tray. Prick the dough all over with a fork and bake for 15 minutes.

Drain most of the liquid from the cooled apples. Spoon the apple filling over the baked dough.

Remove the dough from the freezer and coarsely grate it, as you would cheese. Sprinkle the grated dough over the apples. Return the tray to the oven for 45 minutes until the top of the cake is nicely golden.

Leave the cake to cool in the tray. Dust with confectioners' sugar and serve with whipped cream, if you like.

CHERRY CRUMBLE CAKE

CIASTO WIŚNIOWE Z KRUSZONKĄ

This is a lovely cake to make with any stone fruits in season: cherries, plums, or apricots are all favorites. I like to include some crushed cardamom, but a teaspoon of ground cinnamon works well, too—or simply use the vanilla on its own. A trip around a fresh food market or picking ripe cherries from the trees always inspires me to come home and bake this cake.

Serves 12

14 oz/400 g fresh cherries

For the crumble topping
scant ½ cup/1¾ oz/50 g all-purpose flour
¼ cup/1¾ oz/50 g unsalted butter, at room temperature
¼ cup/1 oz/30 g confectioners' sugar, plus extra for dusting

For the cake batter
generous ¾ cup/6½ oz/180 g unsalted butter, at room temperature
generous ½ cup/4½ oz/125 g superfine sugar
3 large eggs
1 tsp vanilla extract or vanilla bean paste
seeds from 3 green cardamom pods (optional), crushed
generous 1½ cups/7 oz/200 g self-rising flour
1 tsp baking powder

Preheat the oven to 350°F/180°C. Grease and line an 8 in/20 cm round cake pan or a 9 x 12 in/23 x 30 cm cake pan with parchment paper.

Remove the stems from the cherries, then slice each cherry in half and remove the pit. Keep the cherries to one side.

To make the crumble topping, sift the flour into a large bowl. Add the butter and confectioners' sugar. Using your fingers, rub the butter into the flour and sugar to make a crumb-like mixture, then set to one side.

To make the cake batter, using a stand mixer or a whisk, beat the butter and sugar together until pale and creamy—this takes around 5 minutes. Add the eggs, one by one, mixing well. Add the vanilla and the crushed cardamom seeds, if using. Mix together well. Sift in the self-rising flour and baking powder and gently fold in, using a metal spoon, until all the flour is incorporated.

Pour the batter into the lined pan and smooth down with the back of a spoon. Scatter the cherries over the batter and gently press down. Scatter the crumble topping over the cherries. Bake for 55–60 minutes, or until a skewer inserted into the center of the cake comes out clean.

Leave the cake to cool in the pan. Before serving, dust with confectioners' sugar.

The cake will keep well in a cake tin for up to 2 days.

PLUM AND POPPYSEED CAKE

CIASTO ZE ŚLIWKAMI I MAKIEM

If I had to choose a signature bake, this would be it. It is probably one of the easiest cakes you'll ever make, made to a sponge cake recipe that I remember calling my mom up for when I first moved out. In England, I use fresh Victoria plums when they are in season, but any ripe plums will work as well. Sweet plums are plentiful in Poland and the addition of poppyseeds here adds a Polish twist. I once made this for a Polish-inspired pop-up, served with Polish plum martini (page 199).

Serves 12

generous 1 cup/8 oz/225 g
    superfine sugar
4 large eggs, lightly beaten
1 cup/250 ml light vegetable oil,
    preferably organic
1 tsp vanilla extract or vanilla
    bean paste
1 tsp grated orange or lemon zest
2 cups/9 oz/250 g self-rising flour
1 tsp baking powder
3 tbsp poppyseeds
8–10 ripe plums, halved and pitted
2 tbsp confectioners' sugar, mixed
    with 1 tsp ground cinnamon, for
    dusting

Preheat the oven to 350°F/180°C. Grease and line a 9 x 12 in/ 23 x 30 cm sheet cake pan with parchment paper.

In a large bowl, combine the superfine sugar, beaten eggs, oil, and vanilla, and whisk together for 5 minutes, until pale and fluffy. Add the orange or lemon zest and mix again.

Sift in the flour and baking powder and gently fold in, using a metal spoon, until all the flour is incorporated. Sprinkle in the poppyseeds and mix again.

Pour the batter into the lined tray and gently press the halved plums into the batter. Bake for 40 minutes or until a skewer inserted into the center comes out clean.

Leave to cool in the pan. Before serving, dust with the cinnamon-flavored confectioners' sugar.

The cake will keep well in a cake tin in a cool place for up to 4 days.

BLUEBERRY CRUMBLE SQUARES

KRUCHY PLACEK Z JAGODAMI

Blueberries and bilberries are plentiful in Poland. This is a lovely way to use up a seasonal glut ahead of having friends over for tea.

Makes 9 squares

3½ cups/1 lb 2 oz/500 g fresh
  blueberries or wild bilberries

For the pastry
2 cups/9 oz/250 g all-purpose flour,
  plus extra for dusting
1¼ cups/5½ oz/150 g
  confectioners' sugar
generous ½ cup/4½ oz/125 g
  unsalted butter, cold
pinch of salt
2 egg yolks

For the crumble topping
scant ½ cup/1¾ oz/50 g all-
  purpose flour
¼ cup/1¾ oz/50 g unsalted butter,
  at room temperature
¼ cup/1 oz/30 g confectioners'
  sugar, plus extra for dusting
3½ oz/100 g marzipan, grated

Preheat the oven to 350°F/180°C. Grease and line a 9 in/23 cm square cake pan with parchment paper.

Put all the ingredients for the pastry in a food processor or a big bowl. Process or mix with a fork until the ingredients come together. Tip the dough out onto a floured work surface. Knead by hand for 2 minutes, just long enough to bring the dough together. Wrap in plastic wrap and leave to rest in the fridge for 20 minutes.

To make the crumble topping, sift the flour into a large bowl. Add the butter and confectioners' sugar. Using your fingers, rub the butter into the flour and sugar to make a crumb-like mixture, then set to one side.

On a floured work surface, lightly roll out the pastry to about ¼ in/5 mm thick and press it into the bottom of the lined pan. Prick the pastry lightly with a fork and place in the oven to bake for 15 minutes.

Remove the pan from the oven. Layer the blueberries or bilberries over the pastry. Scatter over the grated marzipan and the crumble topping. Bake for 20 minutes until lightly golden brown on top. Leave to cool in the pan, then cut into squares.

The squares will keep well in a cake tin for up to 2 days.

APRICOT AND ALMOND CAKE

CIASTO MORELOWO MIGDAŁOWE

I also make this cake with rhubarb, when in season. It works very well as a gluten-free cake too, using almond flour.

Serves 12

1¼ cups/9 oz/250 g superfine
  sugar
4 large eggs
1 cup/250 ml vegetable oil,
  preferably organic
1 tsp almond extract
grated zest of 1 orange or lemon
generous 1½ cups/7 oz/200 g
  self-rising flour or almond flour
1 tsp baking powder
scant ½ cup/1½ oz/40 g ground
  almonds
9 oz/250 g fresh apricots, halved,
  pitted
confectioners' sugar, for dusting

Preheat the oven to 350°F/180°C. Grease and line a 9 x 12 in/ 23 x 30 cm sheet cake pan with parchment paper.

In a stand mixer or using an electric mixer, beat the superfine sugar and eggs together for 5 minutes, until pale and creamy. Slowly pour in the oil, beating well. Add the almond extract and the orange or lemon zest and mix again.

Sift in the flour and baking powder, and gently fold in, using a metal spoon, until all the flour is incorporated. Add the ground almonds and gently combine.

Pour the batter into the baking tray. Scatter the apricots over the batter and gently press down, leaving some of the fruit visible. Bake for 45 minutes, or until a skewer inserted into the center comes out clean.

Leave to cool in the pan. Dust with confectioners' sugar and cut into squares or slices.

The cake will keep well in a cake tin for up to 4 days.

APPLE PANCAKES

RACUCHY

A simple Polish teatime treat, my children love these as an occasional after-school snack with friends. When I was growing up we used to eat pancakes with plenty of confectioners' sugar, but I now prefer to serve them with a little drizzle of maple syrup or agave nectar. You can make these pancakes with a gluten-free flour blend and almond milk.

Makes 12 pancakes

2 eggs, separated
1 cup/4½ oz/125 g self-rising flour,
　or a gluten-free blend
1 cup/250 ml whole milk
　or almond milk
2 tbsp sugar
2 tsp ground cinnamon
pinch of salt
2 tbsp sour cream
4 small apples or 2 large apples,
　peeled, cored, and finely sliced
2 tbsp vegetable oil, for frying
maple syrup or confectioners'
　sugar, to serve

In a large bowl, mix together the egg yolks, flour, milk, sugar, cinnamon, and salt until well combined. Stir in the sour cream.

In a very clean, dry, metal or glass bowl, whisk the egg whites until stiff. Add the egg whites to the egg yolk mixture and fold in using a metal spoon. Gently stir in the apple slices.

In a large frying pan, heat 1 tablespoon oil over medium heat. Spoon some of the batter into the pan to make palm-sized pancakes—two or three should fit in the pan without touching.

Fry the pancakes on one side for about 2 minutes, until golden brown, then flip over to cook the other side. Transfer to a warmed plate and repeat until you have used up all the batter. Add the remaining tablespoon of oil to the pan halfway through.

Serve the pancakes hot, with a drizzle of maple syrup or a dusting of confectioners' sugar.

CREPES WITH SWEET CREAM CHEESE

NALEŚNIKI Z SEREM

Think of these as a cross between a cheesecake and a pancake. The filling is simply divine! Serve with plenty of fresh fruit—my favorite is blueberries—and a drizzle of maple syrup. You can make these with coconut flour and coconut milk or almond flour and almond milk as a gluten-free or dairy-free alternative.

Makes 6 pancakes

½ cup/2 oz/60 g all-purpose flour,
    coconut flour, or almond flour
2 eggs, separated
⅔ cup/150 ml whole milk, coconut
    milk, or almond milk
1 tsp vanilla extract or vanilla
    bean paste
grated zest of 1 lemon
1 tbsp vegetable oil or coconut oil,
    for frying

For the filling
7 oz/200 g *twaróg*, farmer's
    cheese, cream cheese, or dairy-
    free cream cheese
1 egg yolk
2 tbsp sugar
1 tsp vanilla extract or vanilla
    bean paste

To serve
maple syrup or confectioners'
    sugar, and fruit of your choice

Make the filling first. If the cheese isn't completely smooth, push it through a fine sieve using the back of a spoon. Whisk the egg yolk with the sugar and vanilla until creamy, and then stir in the cheese. The filling should be the consistency of whipped cream. Set to one side.

To make the pancake batter, sift the flour into a large bowl, add the egg yolks, milk, vanilla, and lemon zest, and mix everything together very well.

In a very clean, dry, glass or metal bowl, whisk the egg whites until stiff, and then gently fold into the pancake batter using a metal spoon. Cover with plastic wrap and set aside for about 15 minutes. Mix well before using.

Heat the oil in a large frying pan over a high heat. As soon as the pan is very hot, pour in a ladleful of batter and quickly swirl the pan so that the base of the pan is thinly covered with batter. Cook for 2 minutes and then flip or turn the pancake over and cook the other side for a further 2 minutes. Repeat until all the batter has been used. Keep the pancakes warm on a covered plate while you cook the rest.

Fill each pancake with a spoonful of the sweet cream cheese filling, drizzle with maple syrup or dust with confectioners' sugar, and serve with fresh fruit.

MINI LEMON BABKAS

BABECZKI CYTRYNOWE DO ŚWIĘCONKI

In Poland, a babka is a cake, similar to a brioche, traditionally made with yeast and eaten at Easter. Original babka recipes use yeast as a way of helping the cake to rise. However, as I tend not to bake with yeast very often, I use a light cake flour and a little baking powder, and beat the mixture well to incorporate lots of air. I like to make mini versions of the traditional Easter babka.

You can, of course, make a babka at any time of the year and there are many variations you can play around with, adding, for example, dried fruit or poppyseeds. Typically, babkas are glazed with confectioners' sugar but here I've included a quick white chocolate glaze, which goes well with the lemon-flavored babka. I use two mini bundt pans, each with four molds, but you could make this in one large 8½ in/22 cm diameter bundt pan—a deep cake pan with a hollow center.

Makes 8 small cakes

spray oil, for greasing
1 cup/7 oz/200 g superfine sugar
4 eggs
¼ cup/1¾ oz/50 g butter, at room
   temperature
¼ cup/60 ml vegetable oil
grated zest of 1 lemon
½ cup/4½ oz/125 g plain yogurt
2¼ cups/10 oz/280 g "00" pasta
   flour or cake flour
1 tsp baking powder
pinch of salt

For the white chocolate icing
6 oz/175 g white chocolate or
   white chocolate chips
¼ cup/60 ml heavy cream
3–4 tbsp poppyseeds, for
   sprinkling (optional)

Preheat the oven to 350°F/180°C. Spray the mini bundt pans with oil.

Put the superfine sugar, eggs, butter, and oil into a large bowl and whisk together well for 5 minutes, until pale and fluffy. Add the lemon zest and yogurt and mix again.

Sift in the flour, baking powder, and salt, and gently fold in, using a metal spoon, until all the flour is incorporated. Carefully pour the mixture into the mini bundt pans.

Bake for 20–30 minutes, or until the cakes are a light golden color and a toothpick inserted into the center comes out clean. Leave the babkas to cool in the pans. Turn out when cool enough to handle.

To make the icing, put the white chocolate chips and cream into a bowl set over a saucepan with 2 in/5 cm of gently boiling water. When melted, stir gently until smooth, then drizzle the glaze over the cooled babkas. Sprinkle with poppyseeds, if using, for added texture and color. Leave the icing to set for about 30 minutes before serving.

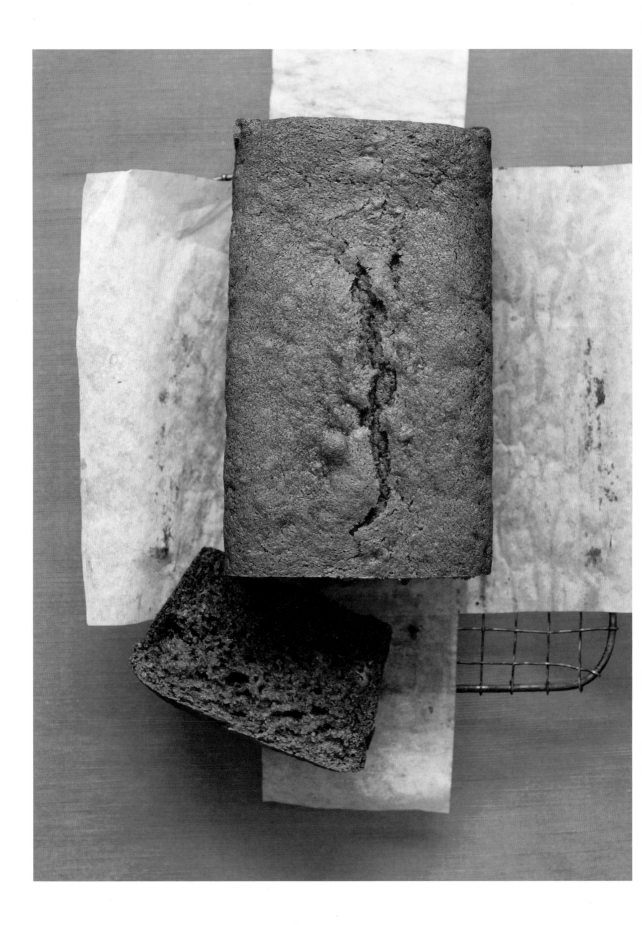

HONEY AND BANANA LOAF CAKE

CIASTO BANANOWE Z MIODEM

I love Polish gingerbread cake, which is very rich in honey and spices and often layered with a thick plum or damson jam called *powidła*. This is a slightly alternative version, still made with honey and spices but with the addition of some very ripe bananas. For a teatime treat, we like to spread a thin layer of butter over slices of this loaf cake, adding a spoonful of plum conserve or damson jam. You can experiment with the honey in this recipe—I like to use raw wildflower honey to add a lovely floral note.

Makes 1 loaf

⅔ cup/5½ oz/150 g margarine
   or butter, softened, plus extra
   for greasing
⅔ cup/5 oz/140 g soft
   brown sugar
2 tbsp clear honey
2 large eggs, at room temperature
1¾ cups/8 oz/225 g self-rising flour
1 tsp ground ginger
1 tsp ground cinnamon
1 tsp pumpkin pie spice
1 tsp baking soda
½ tsp salt
2 overripe bananas, mashed
   (6½ oz/180 g mashed weight)
¼ cup/60 ml sour cream

Preheat the oven to 350°F/180°C. Grease a 2 lb/900 g loaf pan (about 5½ x 9 x 3 in/13 x 23 x 7 cm) and line with parchment paper.

In a stand mixer, beat the margarine or butter with the sugar, honey, and eggs for 3 minutes, until creamy. Sift in the dry ingredients and beat for 1 minute, until just combined. Stir in the bananas and then the sour cream.

Pour the batter into the lined pan and bake for 1½ hours—covering with foil after 20 minutes—or until a skewer inserted into the center comes out clean. Leave the cake in the pan to cool.

Serve in thick slices with butter and Polish plum butter (page 44).

The cake will keep well in a cake tin for up to 4 days.

CELEBRATION TORTE WITH FRESH FRUIT

TORT Z OWOCAMI

A torte is a layered cake filled with whipped cream, pastry cream, or a flavored cream or mousse. Poppyseeds may be added to the cake, making a *tort makowy*, and chopped nuts can be used to decorate the sides. Very often, seasonal fruit will influence the cake, so you may layer with raspberries, strawberries, cherries, or peaches. The sponge cake is soaked in fruit syrup, alcohol, or coffee. Each sponge cake makes two layers when split. If you make both the vanilla and chocolate cakes, you will have four layers.

Serves 10

For the vanilla sponge cake
5 eggs, separated
generous ¾ cup/6 oz/175 g
     superfine sugar
2 tbsp vegetable oil
1 tsp vanilla extract or vanilla
     bean paste
¾ cup/3¼ oz/90 g all-purpose
     flour, or preferably "00" flour
     or cake flour
3 tbsp potato flour
     or almond flour
½ tsp baking powder
grated zest of ½ lemon
2 tbsp whole milk

For the chocolate sponge cake
5 eggs, separated
generous ¾ cup/6 oz/175 g
     superfine sugar
2 tbsp vegetable oil
1 tsp vanilla extract or vanilla
     bean paste
¾ cup/3¼ oz/90 g all-purpose
     flour, or preferably "00" flour or
     cake flour
3 tbsp potato flour
     or almond flour
½ tsp baking powder
2–3 tsp cocoa powder
2 tbsp whole milk

Preheat the oven to 350°F/180°C. The method is the same for the vanilla and chocolate sponges—make them separately. Line a 9 in/23 cm springform cake pan with parchment paper.

In a stand mixer, beat the egg yolks with the sugar until creamy—this takes around 5 minutes. Gently pour in the oil, add the vanilla, and beat for a further 2 minutes. Sift in the flours, baking powder, and lemon zest or cocoa powder. Fold the ingredients together gently with a metal spoon until fully incorporated. Add the milk to loosen the mixture.

Put the egg whites in a very clean, dry, glass or metal bowl and whisk until stiff.

Fold the egg whites into the cake batter until fully incorporated.

Pour the mixture into the lined pan and bake for 30 minutes, or until a thin skewer or toothpick inserted into the center comes out clean.

Leave to cool in the pan for 5 minutes and then turn the cake out onto a wire rack. Leave to cool completely.

When cool, carefully cut each cake horizontally in half.

To make the filling, whisk the cream in a bowl, gradually adding the confectioners' sugar. Put the chocolate into a small bowl set over a saucepan containing 2 in/5 cm of gently boiling water and leave until melted. Stir briefly, then stir the melted chocolate into the cream.

To assemble, brush one layer of sponge cake with about a third of the fruit syrup or liqueur, as evenly as you can. Spread a quarter of the cream over the cake. Arrange some of the fruit on top.

Continued_

_Continued

Place a second layer of sponge cake on top and repeat the process, then repeat with a third layer of sponge cake. Top with the final layer of sponge cake. Cover this with the remaining cream, and then decorate the top with fruit.

Store in a covered container in the fridge until ready to serve.

For the filling

2½ cups/600 ml heavy or whipping cream

scant 1¼ cups/5 oz/140 g confectioners' sugar

3½ oz/100 g white chocolate, broken up

2 tbsp fruit syrup or liqueur, such as vodka or amaretto

14 oz/400 g fresh fruit, such as strawberries, raspberries, sliced plums—or canned sliced peaches

•

POLISH FUDGE ICE CREAM

LODY KRÓWKOWE

Krówki (individually wrapped pieces of Polish fudge) were my favorite Polish candies when I was a child. They were sold behind the bar at the Polish Ex-Combatants Club in Manchester and I felt really grown up being given a few pennies to go up to the bar and buy them. *Krówki* means "little cows" and the packaging often had little cows on it. *Katarzynki*, chocolate-coated gingerbread cookies, were another favorite. I still buy *krówki* and my children love them, too. We have also discovered that if you buy a small can of *masa krówkowa*—which is sold in jars at Polish shops—you can make a very simple and tasty ice cream. (Dulce de leche is very similar.) We like to drench ours with chocolate sauce. You can finely chop some of the crumbly *krówki* candies, too, as a topping.

Makes 4 cups/1 liter

1¾ cups/18 oz/510 g *masa krówkowa* or dulce de leche caramel sauce

2½ cups/600 ml heavy cream

Mix the caramel and the cream together with a spoon and then beat with an electric mixer until thick, but not as thick as butter—you should still be able to move a spoon through it. Pour into a container and cover with plastic wrap or a lid. Freeze until solid.

Serve with chocolate sauce and/or chopped fudge pieces, if you like.

CARAMEL AND CHERRY CHEESECAKE

SERNIK Z MASĄ KRÓWKOWĄ I CZEREŚNIAMI

You can never have too many party cheesecake recipes. This one was inspired by one of my favorite recipes from Polish blogger and author Eliza Mórawska, whose blog is called whiteplate.com. In her book *White Plate Sweet*, Liska shares a recipe for a caramel raspberry cheesecake called *sernikotoffii*. I add a base, and use either raspberries or sweet cherries, when in season. The recipe calls for a caramel sauce called *masa krówkowa*, which you can usually find in the baking section of larger Polish delis. Alternatively, you could use dulce de leche, which is very similar. I have also had good results with cookie butter (like Lotus Biscoff cookie butter) or speculoos spread.

Serves 16

For the crust
2 cups/9 oz/250 g all-purpose flour
scant ½ cup/3½ oz/100 g butter,
    at room temperature
scant ½ cup/3 oz/85 g superfine
    sugar
2 egg yolks

For the caramel layer
scant ½ cup/3½ oz/100 g butter,
    at room temperature
1 egg
¾ cup/9 oz/250 g *masa krówkowa*
    or dulce de leche caramel sauce
2 tbsp cornstarch or potato starch
½ tsp baking powder

For the cheesecake filling
1 cup/7 oz/200 g superfine sugar
2 whole eggs, plus 2 egg whites
14 oz/400 g *twaróg sernikowy*,
    farmer's cheese, or cream cheese
1 tbsp cornstarch or potato starch
generous 1 cup/5½ oz/150
    g cherries, pitted, or fresh
    raspberries

Preheat the oven to 350°F/180°C. Grease and line a 9 x 12 in/ 23 x 30 cm sheet cake pan with parchment paper.

To make the crust, process the flour, butter, sugar, and egg yolks in a food processor. Tip the mixture into the lined tray and press down, using the back of a spoon, until relatively flat. Bake for 15 minutes, until golden. Remove from the oven and leave to cool.

To make the caramel layer, use a stand mixer or electric mixer to beat the butter until creamy. Add the egg and beat again. Add the caramel sauce and mix until smooth. Sift in the cornstarch or potato starch and baking powder, and mix well. Pour this evenly over the cooled crust and smooth down with a spatula.

To make the cheesecake filling, beat the sugar and the whole eggs together until creamy. Mix in the farmer's cheese or cream cheese, and cornstarch or potato starch. In a very clean, dry, glass or metal bowl, whisk the egg whites until stiff and then fold them into the sugar and egg mixture using a metal spoon. Pour the cheesecake mixture—which will be quite loose—over the caramel layer and stud with the cherries or raspberries.

Bake the cheesecake for 45 minutes. It should be golden on top and still a little wobbly to the touch. If it appears to be getting too brown after 30 minutes, cover it with foil.

Once cooked, switch the oven off and open the door, but leave the cheesecake in the oven. After 1 hour or so, take the cheesecake out of the oven, leave it to cool completely, and then transfer to the fridge overnight. This is best served chilled.

POLISH CHEESECAKE WITH RAISINS

SERNIK Z RODZYNKAMI

A typical Polish cheesecake is baked and sits on a pastry crust rather than a graham cracker crust. This is a dense cheesecake, to be served in small slices. The addition of raisins is lovely, adding a little moisture; when baked, the raisins almost caramelize—delicious. I love this cheesecake for its delicate texture and elegance—quite unusual for an Eastern European baked dessert! The Polish way to serve cheesecake is with a delicate cup of lemon tea. The best Polish cheesecake I had recently was in a café with beautiful exposed brick walls, right by the Chopin Museum in Warsaw. The perfect end to a busy afternoon.

Serves 16

For the crust
2 cups/9 oz/250 g all-purpose flour, plus extra for dusting
scant ½ cup/3½ oz/100 g butter, at room temperature
scant ½ cup/3 oz/85 g sugar
2 egg yolks

For the filling
1 lb 5 oz/600 g *twaróg sernikowy*, farmer's cheese, or cream cheese
⅔ cup/5½ oz/150 g unsalted butter, at room temperature
1¼ cups/9 oz/250 g superfine sugar
6 eggs, separated
1¼ cups/7 oz/200 g raisins
grated zest of ½ lemon
1 tsp vanilla extract or vanilla bean paste
1 tbsp potato starch or cornstarch

Preheat the oven to 350°F/180°C. Grease and line a 9 x 12 in/ 23 x 30 cm sheet cake pan with parchment paper.

To make the crust, process the flour, butter, sugar, and egg yolks in a food processor. Tip the mixture into the lined tray and press it down, using the back of a tablespoon or the palm of your hand, until flat. Bake for 15 minutes, until golden. Remove from the oven and leave to cool while you make the filling.

To make the filling, if the farmer's cheese isn't completely smooth, push it through a fine sieve using the back of a spoon. Beat the butter with the sugar, until pale and creamy. Beat in the egg yolks, one at a time. Add the cheese and beat again.

In a very clean, dry, glass or metal bowl, whisk the egg whites until stiff and then fold them into the butter and sugar mixture using a metal spoon. Stir in the raisins, lemon zest, and vanilla. Finally, stir in the potato starch or cornstarch.

Pour the cheesecake mixture over the crust and return it to the oven. Bake for 1 hour—covering with foil after 40 minutes. It should be golden on top and still a little wobbly to the touch. Switch the oven off and open the door, but leave the cheesecake in the oven.

After 1 hour or so, take the cheesecake out of the oven and leave it to cool completely, then transfer to the fridge overnight. This is best served chilled.

POLISH SPICED CHRISTMAS COOKIES

PIERNICZKI ŚWIĄTECZNE

These Christmas cookies very quickly became the most popular recipe on my website when I first posted them in November 2011, just a year into starting my food blog. Since then, I've loved receiving emails and photos of the cookies that friends and readers have made for their own trees, or to give as gifts around the holidays. Instead of making the icing to decorate the cookies, you could buy ready-made cookie icing. Since I use wild honey and rye (flour) in my cookies, the title of my book was hidden within this recipe—long before I knew it!

Makes about 24 cookies, depending on the size of cutters used

½ cup/4 oz/115 g unsalted butter, plus extra for greasing
½ cup/4 oz/115 g soft dark brown sugar
½ cup/125 ml clear honey
3½ cups/1 lb/450 g all-purpose flour or rye flour, plus extra for dusting
2 tsp baking powder
2 tsp ground ginger
2 tsp ground cinnamon
2 tbsp mixed spice
2 tbsp cocoa powder
1 egg

To decorate
1¼ cups/5½ oz/150 g confectioners' sugar, sifted
1 egg white
1 tbsp water
food coloring (optional)

Preheat the oven to 400°F/200°C. Lightly grease three large baking sheets with butter.

Put the butter, brown sugar, and honey in a small saucepan over low heat. Stir only until the butter has melted. Set to one side.

In a large bowl, sift the dry ingredients together, mix well, add the egg, and mix again. Pour the melted butter mixture into the dry ingredients and stir until the dough starts to come together.

Tip the mixture out onto a lightly floured work surface and knead to form a ball. If the mixture is too crumbly, add a tablespoon of water at a time and knead again until it comes together. Roll out the dough to about ⅛ in/3 mm. Cut out shapes using cookie cutters and carefully lift the cookies onto the baking sheets; leave about ¾ in/1–2 cm around each cookie—they don't spread too much. Bake the cookies for 7–8 minutes per batch, until golden.

While the cookies are baking, make the icing by stirring together the confectioners' sugar, egg white, and water. If you like, divide the icing into different bowls and add a little food coloring to one or more bowls. Mix together really well until you have a thick paste that will pour evenly off a spoon. Fill a pastry bag fitted with a fine tip with the icing and set to one side.

When the cookies are baked, they will still be a bit soft. Using a palette knife, carefully lift them onto a wire rack and leave to cool. If you are decorating the cookies for the tree, use a chopstick to make a small hole in the top of each cookie as soon as they come out of the oven, but be careful not to break the top off the cookie by pressing too hard.

Once cooled, decorate your cookies with the icing. Store in a cookie tin for up to 2 weeks, since they will soften. If used as Christmas tree decorations, they can be left on the tree for the season.

FRUIT LIQUEURS AND FLAVORED VODKAS

NALEWKI I WÓDKI

A whole chapter on flavored vodka—and why not? Some say that vodka was invented in Poland. The word derives from *woda*, meaning water. Adding the diminutive *ka* to the end of a word in Polish makes something little, hence *wódka* means "little water." In Poland, you may come across a type of vodka-based drink called a *nalewka* (plural *nalewki*), which is made to a very specific method: it involves macerating fruit or, sometimes, herbs and spices, in very strong alcohol—usually *spirytus rectyfikowany*, or rectified spirit—and then later straining the fruit, adding sugar, and then vodka to dilute the resulting liqueur. This is a slightly different process to making *schnapps*, or other flavored vodkas, when you usually add the sugar to the fruit and then top that up with vodka or other alcohol. A *nalewka* is thus a much stronger liqueur and it is usually defined by the aging and clarifying process, which happens over at least six months.

If you visit a Pole in their home, they will likely offer you a glass (or two) of their own homemade *nalewka*, which you should sip, rather than drink it as you might a cold shot. Be aware that it is likely to be very high in alcohol. When we visit my Aunt Zosia and Uncle Władek in Wrocław they offer us their homemade *wiśniówka*, a cherry-flavored vodka. And my good friend Monika always returns from Poland with a bottle or two in her suitcase, made by her dad, Lech.

The name given to a *nalewka* is usually derived from the ingredient from which it is made; if you make a *nalewka* from cherries, or *wiśnie*, you would call this *wiśniówka*. Apricots in Polish are *morele*, hence an apricot *nalewka* might be called *morelówka*, or a *nalewka morelowa*.

The flavored vodkas later in the chapter cannot strictly be described as *nalewki*, since they are not aged. I tend to make them with soft fruits, when I want a quicker, lighter result.

A word of extreme caution: in most cases, to make a traditional *nalewka*, you would use *spirytus rectyfikowany* or *spirytus nalewkowy*—rectified spirit, bottled at 95% ABV (alcohol by volume) or 190 proof. This is a base, which you later mix with a normal-strength (40% ABV, 80 proof) vodka. You should never drink *spirytus* neat. If you are afraid of using rectified spirit, or can't find any (it is banned in some countries!), use the highest strength and best quality vodka you can find.

If you make your *nalewka* with seasonal fruits in the summer, it will be ready in time for the first star—meaning Christmas Eve (ahem, traditionally an evening that doesn't involve strong liquor).

TRADITIONAL FRUIT LIQUEUR

NALEWKI NA SPIRYTUSIE ZE ŚWIEŻYCH OWOCÓW

This is a traditional method of making a fruit *nalewka*. You can use most stone fruit for this method, such as cherries, apricots, or plums. You could also use quince, pears, or apples. For plum vodka, called *śliwowica*, Poles use a type of purple plum called *śliwki węgierki*. You can also use this method for soft fruits, but you will only need to macerate the fruit for 2–3 weeks before leaving the *nalewka* to age. The fruit should be ripe, but not overripe. Cut around any blemishes/insect holes.

I'll repeat my word of caution about using *spirytus*—never drink it neat. If you can't find any *spirytus rectyfikowany* (rectified spirit, 95% ABV, 190 proof), use a good-quality clear vodka (40% ABV, 80 proof).

A note on pits: usually, the pits are removed before the spirit is poured over the fruit. Some people like to add a handful of pits, since they impart a very particular flavor. However, if you leave them in for too long they can impart a bitter flavor. A tip from Monika's dad, Lech, is to wrap a few pits in a piece of cheesecloth and then clip them to the top of the jar, submerged in spirit, making it much easier for you to take them out after about a week.

Makes 1½–2 quarts/1.5–2 liters

2¼ lb/1 kg stone fruit, such as
   cherries, plums, or apricots
4 cups/1 liter *spirytus rectyfikowany*
   (rectified spirit)—or use
   2 cups/500 ml rectified spirit
   plus 2 cups/500 ml good-quality
   vodka, or 4 cups/1 liter vodka
2½ cups/1 lb 2 oz/500 g sugar—if
   the fruit is very sweet or ripe, you
   can try using less sugar, perhaps
   half the amount
about 2 cups/500 ml
   good-quality vodka—or a 750
   ml bottle—will be needed at the
   end of the process to dilute
   the liqueur

Step One
Sterilize a half-gallon/2-liter preserving jar (see page 207). Wash the fruit and remove the pits. Retain about half of the pits and tie them in a small piece of cheesecloth. Place all the fruit into the jar. Pour over the rectified spirit and/or vodka, submerge the wrapped pits, and seal the jar. Leave to infuse in a cool, dark place for 4–6 weeks, shaking the jar every day or so. Remove the pits after a week or so.

Step Two
Sterilize two additional 2-quart/2-liter jars. Place a cheesecloth-lined sieve over one of the jars, and strain the spirit. Put the strained fruit into the other jar and add the sugar. Seal and leave in a cool dark place for 2–3 weeks, shaking every now and again.

Seal the jar of spirit and set aside—do not drink this.

Step Three
After 2–3 weeks, the sugar in the fruit jar will have dissolved. The resulting liquid is an alcoholic fruit syrup. Strain the fruit, pouring the syrup into the jar of spirit that you had previously saved. Shake well. Seal the jar and store it for as long as possible, ideally for 6 months.

The strained, alcohol-infused fruit can be spooned over ice cream or added to a cake.

Continued_

_Continued

Step Four
After a good few months, now that the *nalewka* has aged, dilute with 2–3 cups/500–700 ml normal-strength vodka and taste it. It should be sweet, strong, and very alcoholic. Serve or decant into bottles.

Sip at room temperature. Or serve in a tall glass topped up with ice and soda water or lemonade for a long drink.

QUINCE VODKA
PIGWÓWKA

Use 2¼ lb/1 kg quince, peeled and chopped, in place of the stone fruit.

RHUBARB AND VANILLA VODKA
RABARBARÓWKA Z WANILIĄ

2 lb 12 oz/1.2 kg or 8 sticks of fresh rhubarb
2 vanilla beans
4 cups/1 liter *spirytus rectyfikowany* (rectified spirit)—or use 2 cups/ 500 ml rectified spirit plus 2 cups/500 ml good-quality vodka, or 4 cups/1 liter vodka
2½ cups/1 lb 2 oz/500 g granulated sugar
about 2 cups/500 ml good-quality vodka—or use a 750 ml bottle

Trim the rhubarb and discard any soft ends. Chop into ¾ in/2 cm pieces. Put the rhubarb into a large sterilized jar (see page 207), along with the vanilla, cover with rectified spirit and/or vodka, and then seal the jar. Leave to macerate in a cool, dark place for 2 weeks.

Follow Steps Two and Three of the method for the Traditional fruit liqueur. After Step Three, you can purée the strained rhubarb, pass it through a sieve, and use it to flavor cocktails—see the Polish plum martini on page 199.

Follow Step Four, diluting with 2–3 cups/500–700 ml vodka before serving or storing.

CHERRY VODKA
WIŚNIÓWKA

This is a quicker way to make cherry vodka: you only have to wait about a month (rather than six months) before this is ready.

Makes about 4 cups/1 liter

1 lb 2 oz/500 g cherries, halved, keeping the pits
½ cup/3½ oz/100 g granulated sugar
1 bottle (750 ml) good-quality vodka (at least 40% ABV, 80 proof)
1 cinnamon stick (optional)

Sterilize a 1.5-liter preserving jar (see page 207). Put the cherries and sugar in the jar and lightly crush the cherries with the sugar. Pour over the vodka. Tie up the cherry pits in a small piece of cheesecloth. Immerse the pits and, if using, the cinnamon stick in the vodka and seal the jar. Leave to infuse in a cool, dark place.

After a week, remove the pits. Seal again, shake, and leave to infuse in a cool, dark place for at least a month.

Strain through a cheesecloth-lined sieve and decant into a bottle.

REDCURRANT VODKA
NALEWKA Z CZERWONEJ PORZECZKI

Makes about 4 cups/1 liter

1 lb 2 oz/500 g redcurrants
¼ cup/60 ml clear honey
1 bottle (750 ml) good-quality vodka (at least 40% ABV, 80 proof)

Wash the redcurrants, remove the stalks, and place in a sterilized 1 quart/1-liter preserving jar (see page 207). Add the honey and lightly crush the redcurrants. Pour over the vodka, seal the jar, and shake. Leave to infuse in a cool, dark place for 2–4 weeks. Strain the vodka into a bottle. Serve chilled, preferably from the freezer.

RASPBERRY VODKA
MALINÓWKA

Makes about 4 cups/1 liter

2¼ lb/1 kg raspberries
2 cups/500 ml clear honey
1 bottle (750 ml) good-quality vodka (at least 40% ABV, 80 proof)

Wash the raspberries and place them in a sterilized 2-liter preserving jar (see page 207). Pour in the honey and vodka and seal the jar. Leave to infuse in a cool, dark place for 4–6 weeks. Shake well every 2–3 days.

Strain the vodka though a cheesecloth-lined sieve into a clean jar. (You can use the macerated fruit for puddings or to top ice cream.) Keep the vodka in a cool, dark place for another 2 weeks.

Strain the vodka once more to make sure it is very clear—this time into 2 clean bottles.

BLACKBERRY VODKA
NALEWKA Z JEŻYN

Makes about 4 cups/1 liter

2¼ lb/1 kg blackberries
1¼ cups/9 oz/250 g granulated sugar
1 bottle (750 ml) good-quality vodka (at least 40% ABV, 80 proof)

Wash the blackberries and place them in a sterilized ½ gallon or 1.5-liter preserving jar (see page 207). Add the sugar and lightly crush the berries with the sugar. Pour in the vodka, seal the jar, and shake. Leave to infuse in a cool, dark place for 2–4 weeks.

Strain the vodka into a bottle. Serve chilled, preferably from the freezer.

LEMON VODKA
CYTRYNÓWKA

Makes 750 ml (1 bottle)

1 unwaxed lemon
1 tbsp sugar
1 bottle (750 ml) good-quality vodka (at least 40% ABV, 80 proof)

Peel the zest of the lemon into strips, taking care not to include the white pith. Put the zest into a sterilized 1-quart/1-liter preserving jar (see page 207), add the sugar, and pour in the vodka. Seal the jar, shake well, and leave to infuse for 1 month.

Serve chilled, preferably from the freezer.

Mixed citrus fruit vodka
You can also add some strips of orange or lime zest to create a citrus fruit vodka.

SALTED CARAMEL VODKA
PRZYPALANKA Z SOLĄ MORSKĄ

Makes about 4 cups/1 liter

½ cup/3½ oz/100 g sugar
2 cups/500 ml freshly boiled water
pinch of sea salt
1 bottle (750 ml) good-quality vodka (at least 40% ABV, 80 proof)

Sterilize a 1-quart/1-liter preserving jar (see page 207). Put the sugar into a heavy-based frying pan over low heat. Heat until the sugar has dissolved and turned into a dark caramel—shake the pan from time to time to ensure the sugar caramelizes evenly, but do not stir. Pour in the boiled water (be very careful since it will bubble) and a good pinch of sea salt. Leave to cool.

Pour the caramel into the sterilized jar and pour in the vodka. Leave in a cool, dark place for 2–3 days. If you wish, transfer to a bottle. Shake well before serving.

SPICED HONEY VODKA
KRUPNIK NA SPIRYTUSIE

Krupnik is a type of honey-flavored vodka or liqueur, based on a traditional 17th-century Lithuanian drink called *krupnikas*; you'll sometimes see recipes for *krupnik Litewski*, or Lithuanian krupnik. *Krupnik* is also the name given to a Polish soup made with barley, so take care not to get confused! Traditionally, this drink is served hot, with a pat of butter added.

Makes about 4 cups/1 liter

1 cup/250 ml clear honey, preferably
   raw, wild, or organic
1 cup/250 ml lukewarm water
½ whole nutmeg
1 cinnamon stick
2 allspice berries
½ tsp ground ginger
1 vanilla bean
dried peel of ½ orange
1 bottle (750 ml) good-quality vodka (at least 40% ABV,
   80 proof)
unsalted butter, to serve

Put the honey and warm water into a saucepan, and add the spices and orange peel. Heat gently until boiling, then simmer for 5 minutes. Skim off any foam. Remove from the heat and leave to cool.

Add the vodka and stir well. You can leave this to infuse overnight.

Strain through a cheesecloth-lined sieve and pour into a bottle. Store in a cool, dark place for 2–3 days. Strain again through a cheesecloth-lined sieve and transfer to a fresh bottle.

To serve, heat the *krupnik* gently, and add a little pat of butter to each glass.

POLISH PLUM MARTINI

MARTINI ZE ŚLIWKAMI

My favorite cocktail, which was created for a Polish "pop-up" I ran a few years ago. I teamed up with a local cocktail bar, Mokoko, who created some cocktails to match the recipes I was serving. This martini really stood out and, unusually, it was paired with dessert: Plum and poppyseed cake (page 167) served with cinnamon whipped cream. You can make this cocktail with your own homemade plum vodka or liqueur, or with store-bought *śliwowica*, as plum vodka is called in Poland. The Mokoko boys added plum bitters, though I tend to make a fresh plum purée instead. I like to garnish the glass with a slice of fresh plum and a star anise.

The plum purée and/or a dash of *śliwowica* can also be added to a glass and topped up with champagne for a Polish-style Bellini.

Serves 2

⅔ cup/150 ml good-quality vodka, or use plum-flavored vodka (*śliwowica*)
2 star anise, to garnish

For the plum purée
1 cup/7 oz/200 g sugar
1 cup/250 ml water
9 oz/250 g fresh plums, pitted and sliced

Begin by making a sugar syrup. Put the sugar and water in a saucepan, bring it to a boil, and cook until all the sugar has dissolved, then remove the pan from the heat and leave the syrup to cool completely. You can store this in a sterilized container for up to 1 month.

Set aside two plum slices to garnish. Put the remaining plum slices into a saucepan, cover them with the sugar syrup, and bring to a boil. Simmer until the plums soften, then leave to cool. Pureé the plum mixture in a food processor, then strain through a fine sieve lined with cheesecloth. Place the plum purée in the fridge to chill.

Chill your cocktail shaker and two martini glasses in the freezer for 20 minutes before you start making your cocktails.

Pour the vodka and 4 tablespoons of the plum purée into a cocktail shaker filled with ice. Shake well and strain into two martini glasses. Garnish with a thin slice of plum and a star anise in each glass.

INDEX

ACKNOWLEDGMENTS

In many ways, the final pages of this book have been the hardest ones to write because I am filled with gratitude to a great many people who have championed, inspired, and willed me to write this book. It is so hard to convey my thanks in a few paragraphs. This has, quite simply, been the realization of a very big dream, which I had talked about for many years, not knowing quite how it would come about.

Thank you…

To my husband Ed and children Edward, Elena, and Matthew for loving me and supporting me throughout.

To my parents, to whom this book is dedicated. I thank them for bringing me up with such a deeply embedded respect for Poland, their ancestral homeland. Finally, I get why you sent me to Polish School! Thank you Mama, for always being at the end of the phone to answer my questions on cooking methods and for your industrial-scale pierogi making, buffets, and family gatherings, and for your help with the children when we are together. Although my father is no longer here, he is a man who left behind him a great legacy to fly the flag for Poland even when one is far away.

To my sisters Elizabeth, Wanda, Basia, and brother Roman for their support—there is a recipe for each of you in the book.

To Auntie Anna and Richard and my mother-in-law, Kathy, for your support at home.

To Heather Holden-Brown, my literary agent—how lucky we were to have met at the Guild of Food Writers Award Evening in 2015. I had all but given up on my dreams, yet you immediately acknowledged that the book bubbling away inside me simply had to be written. Thank you for your enthusiasm, belief, advice, and encouragement along the way, and to Cara at HHB Agency, too. I am also grateful to the professional support of the Guild of Food Writers.

This book ultimately happened because of a very forward-thinking and visionary duo— Emily Preece-Morrison and Katie Cowan at Pavilion Books. Thank you for being bold in commissioning a book on Polish food and for giving me this opportunity. I have loved working with you, Emily. Thank you for holding together the very modern direction of this book and for bringing together the hugely talented team for our shoots: the brilliant food photographer Yuki Sugiura, home economist Becci Woods, and assistants (tackling Polish food for the first time!), along with prop stylist extraordinaire Alexander Breeze—thank you all for your creativity and attention to detail. Thank you also to Laura Russell for your amazing talent for design and to Maggie Ramsay for your gentle hand in editing.

I am extremely grateful to the editorial team at JamieOliver.com, to *delicious.* magazine, and to *BBC Good Food* magazine for their support with my recipes and writing and for giving me the opportunity of introducing my Polish food to a wider audience over the last few years.

Thank you to Dianne Jacob across the pond for your advice on the structure of my proposal and for your editing. To one of our best British food writers, Diana Henry, for your earlier words of wisdom and feedback on title ideas. And to Sabrina Ghayour, Olia Hercules, and Grace Cheetham for being incredibly inspirational women, too. To Vanessa Kimbell and Xanthe Clay for a fascinating workshop on "How to Write a Cookery Book"—I listened! Also, Nick Coffer at BBC Three Counties Radio for first airing my Polish dishes on the "Weekend Kitchen" and for suggesting that my food would make for the subject of a very good book almost seven years ago.

To my closest friends from school, Claire, Nicola, Becky, Laura, and Sian, for all your encouragement, and to my closest friends in St. Albans for cups of tea and coffee, recipe testing, and proofreading, Monika, my true Polish friend—*dziękuję*—and to Christina, too. Thank you also to Julie, Herminia, and Andrea for extra playdates and pickups. To Nadia, Melanie, and Lisa for keeping my goals in check. To Michelle at Pink Soul Photography for such inspirational video collaborations, beginning with *Cake Creation* in 2012.

Writing can be lonely at times, so I would also like to thank my food blogging friends for your unwavering support of my work and my blog: many of you have read and commented on my posts since November 2010. I would also like to thank each and every one of my readers at renbehan.com and my supporters online and across social media.

I thank my Polish family, both here and in Poland, particularly to Rysio, Iza, Joasia, Agnieszka, Bozena, and Robert in Warsaw, for your amazing hospitality during our visits.

Also, a huge thank you to the group "Manchester Poles Reunited"—many great friendships have been forged here. To the former Consul General Urszula Gacek for your kind words and encouragement during my visit to the Polish Consulate in New York—I look forward to visiting you and the bees in your garden in Poland soon.

Finally, to my Polish-Mancunian friends, author Bozena Brzeczek (B.E. Andre) and Macmillan and Polish Scouts fundraiser Agnieszka Sheppard, for the impromptu trip to Warsaw, and to Chef Marek Kropielnicki for the food we all shared—without doubt this trip played a part in the direction of this book.

Long may the appreciation of our Polish heritage continue.

NOTES

HOW TO STERILIZE JARS AND BOTTLES

For jams, pickles, and other preserves, I find it easiest to
sterilize the jars and bottles in the dishwasher. Wash the jars and
lids in hot soapy water, place them in the dishwasher, and put
them through the highest heat cycle.

If you don't have a dishwasher, the traditional way is to use the
oven. Heat the oven to 325°F/160°C. Wash the jars and lids
in warm soapy water. Place the jars upside down on a clean baking
tray and place in the oven for 15 minutes. Put lids and rubber
seals in a pan of boiling water and leave to soak.

When filling sterilized jars, use hot jars when filling with hot
preserves such as jam, and cold jars when filling with cold liquids.

•

EGGS

Choose free-range or organic eggs. I tend to use large eggs,
but in most recipes the size won't make much difference.

First American edition published in 2018 by
INTERLINK BOOKS
An imprint of Interlink Publishing Group, Inc.
46 Crosby Street, Northampton, MA 01060
www.interlinkbooks.com

All recipe photography by Yuki Sugiura
Photographs on pages 2, 8, 12, 15, 16-17, 21, 22, 24,
46, 50, 68, 94, 115, 116, 200 © Renatka Behan
Illustration © Shutterstock

Library of Congress Cataloging-in-Publication Data available
ISBN 978-1-62371-998-2

10 9 8 7 6 5 4 3 2 1

Reproduction by Mission, Hong Kong
Printed and bound by 1010 Printing International Ltd, China

To request our 48-page, full-color catalog, please call us toll
free at 1-800-238-LINK, visit www.interlinkbooks.com, or send
us an e-mail at: sales@interlinkbooks.com.